G. SCHIRMER'S COLLECTION OF OPERA LIBRETTOS

DIE MEISTERSINGER VON NÜRNBERG

Opera in Three Acts

Text and Music by
Richard Wagner

English Version by
JOHN GUTMAN

Ed. 2539

G. SCHIRMER, *Inc.*

DISTRIBUTED BY

HAL•LEONARD®

Note

G. SCHIRMER, *Inc.*

DIE MEISTERSINGER

Wagner first considered an opera about Hans Sachs, the historical cobbler-poet of Nuremberg, as early as 1845. (Gustav Albert Lortzing had composed one five years before.) This singing-contest story, thought Wagner, would serve as a comic alternate to the recently completed *Tannhäuser*. *Die Meistersinger* did not materialize, however, until fourteen years later.

The first of the scenarios is dated Marienbad, July 1845, the second, Vienna, October 1861. Both are very detailed; but between the two dates Wagner's conception of his two characters, and of several points in the action, considerably altered. Hans Sachs, from "an unpleasantly ironical character" and not at all a popular one, becomes the wise, human, humorous, yet profoundly melancholy at heart man we now know. Walther, who pleads for pity in Act I of the first sketch, becomes proud and defiant in the second. There is, in the first sketch, no tender relationship between Eva and Sachs: she dislikes and distrusts him; there is no "morning-dream song" in Act III, and Sachs' soliloquy in that act is an ill-tempered outburst about the decadence of poetic art in Germany. Wagner translated the story into its final form—rhymed verse—during a stay in Paris in 1861.

Die Meistersinger was not the first comedy by this serious composer; his first two works, *Die Feen* (based on a fantasy by Carlo Gozzi, who also furnished the original for Puccini's *Turandot*) and *Das Liebesverbot* (after Shakespeare's *Measure for Measure*), treat lighter subjects. To catch the folk mood of *Die Meistersinger*, Wagner used some of the older forms he had renounced in *Tristan* and his half-completed *Ring* cycle, penning a potpourri overture and such set pieces as the Quintet and Prize Song. Nevertheless, the score is distinguished by unity of style and steady musical line.

Its premiere was a popular success (Munich, June 21, 1868, Cosima's erstwhile husband Hans von Bülow conducting), but the critical fraternity, whom Wagner lampooned in the character of Beckmesser, fell upon the fifty-five-year-old composer, who withdrew in disgust to Switzerland to finish the *Ring*. The new work gained hold in a number of German cities, though it did not reach Nuremberg until 1874.

The twelfth production outside Germany took place at the Metropolitan on January 4, 1886, with Anton Seidl conducting a cut version and Emil Fischer as Sachs. Later the DeReske brothers sang it under Damrosch, while Friedrich Schorr became the most famous Sachs in the decades between the World Wars.

J.W.F.

Courtesy Opera News.

THE STORY

ACT I. A young knight, Walther von Stolzing, tries to attract the attention of Eva Pogner as she sits at her devotion with her nurse, Magdalene, in St. Katherine's Church. Services over, Eva tells him she is to be betrothed the next day to the winner of a song contest sponsored by the Mastersingers' Guild. Meanwhile, the apprentice David courts Magdalene. The women leave as other apprentices prepare for a preliminary song trial to be conducted shortly in the church. David tells Walther of his own musical training with the cobbler-poet Hans Sachs and explains the procedures of the contest. When the Mastersingers enter, led by Pogner, Eva's father, Walther asks permission to enter the competition, to the annoyance of the town clerk, Beckmesser, who is also a contestant. Pogner addresses his fellow masters, saying he offers his daughter's hand as proof that tradesmen esteem art. When Sachs suggests that Eva should have some voice in her marriage, Pogner asserts his rules: she may reject the winner but must wed a Mastersinger. Walther sings his trial song, with Beckmesser marking his "errors" on a slate. When the masters join in disapproval, Walther stalks out, leaving Sachs to muse on what he has heard.

ACT II. On Midsummer's Eve, as apprentices playfully end their day's work, David tells Magdalene that Walther was rejected. Eva enters with Pogner, who retires for supper; she remains behind briefly to learn the bad news. Sachs meanwhile sets up a bench in the doorway of his shop; the scent of the lilacs and the memory of Walther's song, however, distract him from his work. Eva visits him, confessing she would be content if he won the contest. The conversation turns to Walther; when Sachs pretends disapproval of the knight, Eva's dismay tells him her true feelings. No sooner does he withdraw than Walther rushes in and impetuously begs Eva to elope with him. They hide as the Nightwatchman passes by. Sachs, who has overheard their plans, places a bright lantern in his window, illuminating the entire street and forcing the lovers to remain in the shadows as Beckmesser arrives to serenade Eva, whom Magdalene impersonates in her window. While the clerk tunes his lute, Sachs launches into a lusty cobbler's song. Beckmesser asks him to stop, but Sachs replies he must finish his work; at length they agree that he will drive a nail only when the pedant's serenade breaks a rule of style. The racket that follows reaches new heights when David jealously attacks Beckmesser for wooing Magdalene, and the neighbors, in their nightshirts, join in a free-for-all. Sachs drags Walther and David into his shop and, at the sound of the Watchman's horn, the throng vanishes, leaving the moonlit street in peace.

ACT III. Reading a book in his study, Sachs hardly hears David apologize for his unruly behavior; the cobbler forgives him and bids him recite his St. John's Day verses. Left alone, Sachs contemplates the madness of a world torn by hate and discord. Walther enters and tells of a wondrous dream; Sachs, recognizing a prize song in the making, takes down his words and instructs him in perfecting the form. After they leave, Beckmesser limps in and pockets the poem; the cobbler catches him in the theft but tells him to keep the paper. Beckmesser joyfully runs out. Eva, hoping to see Walther, comes to Sachs on the pretext that her shoe pinches; the knight soon reenters the room and is inspired to finish his song. Sachs, concealing his emotion, gives the couple his blessing and, when Magdalene joins them, promotes David to journeyman. Led by Eva, they rejoice at the dawning of new love and depart for the contest.

The guilds merrily assemble on a sunny meadow where festive banners wave. The masters file in ceremoniously; when Sachs appears the Nurembergers break into a spontaneous salute, which moves him deeply. The song contest begins as Beckmesser nervously steps forward to sing the poem; but he is plagued by memory lapses and distorts the verse, causing the crowd to burst into laughter. The clerk turns furiously on Sachs, who summons the true author to deliver the poem. Walther wins both Eva and the masters' laurel but refuses their medal, proffered by Pogner. Sachs, however, extolling German art, persuades him to accept the honor. Eva then takes the wreath from Walther's brow and crowns the cobbler-poet as the populace shouts its approval.

Courtesy Opera News.

CAST OF CHARACTERS

HANS SACHS, Shoemaker		Bass
VEIT POGNER, Goldsmith		Bass
KUNZ VOGELGESANG, Furrier		Tenor
KONRAD NACHTIGALL, Tinsmith		Bass
SIXTUS BECKMESSER, Town Clerk		Bass
FRITZ KOTHNER, Baker		Bass
BALTHASAR ZORN, Pewterer	*Mastersingers*	Tenor
ULRICH EISSLINGER, Grocer		Tenor
AUGUSTIN MOSER, Tailor		Tenor
HERMANN ORTEL, Soapmaker		Bass
HANS SCHWARZ, Stocking Weaver		Bass
HANS FOLTZ, Coppersmith		Bass
WALTHER VON STOLZING, a young knight from Franconia		Tenor
DAVID, Sachs' Apprentice		Tenor
EVA, Pogner's Daughter		Soprano
MAGDALENE, Eva's Companion		Mezzo-Soprano
A NIGHTWATCHMAN		Bass

Men and Women of all Guilds, Journeymen, Prentices, Girls, Townspeople.

Nürnberg, 16th Century

SYNOPSIS OF SCENES

DIE MEISTERSINGER VON NÜRNBERG

ERSTER AUFZUG

Die Bühne stellt das Innere der Katharinenkirche in schrägem Durchschnitt dar; von dem Hauptschiff, welches links ab, dem Hintergrunde zu, sich ausdehnend anzunehmen ist, sind nur noch die letzten Reihen der Kirchenstühlbänke sichtbar: den Vordergrund nimmt der freie Raum vor dem Chor ein; dieser wird später durch einen schwarzen Vorhang gegen das Schiff zu gänzlich geschlossen. In der letzten Reihe der Kirchstühle sitzen Eva und Magdalene; Walther von Stolzing steht, in einiger Entfernung, zur Seite an eine Säule gelehnt, die Blicke auf Eva heftend, die sich mit stummem Gebärdenspiel wiederholt zu ihm umkehrt.

DIE GEMEINDE

Da zu dir der Heiland kam,
Willig deine Taufe nahm,
Weihte sich dem Opfertod,
Gab er uns des Heil's Gebot.
Dass wir durch sein' Tauf' uns weih'n,
Seines Opfers wert zu sein.
Edler Täufer!
Christ's Vorläufer!
Nimm uns gnädig an,
Dort am Fluss Jordan.

(Die Gemeinde erhebt sich. Alles wendet sich dem Ausgange zu, und verlässt unter dem Nachspiele allmählich die Kirche. Walther heftet in höchster Spannung seinen Blick auf Eva, welche ihren Sitz ebenfalls verlässt und von Magdalene gefolgt, langsam in seine Nähe kommt.)

WALTHER

Verweilt! Ein Wort! Ein einzig Wort!

EVA *(zu Magdalene)*

Mein Brusttuch! Schau! Wohl liegt's im Ort . . .

MAGDALENE

Vergesslich Kind! Nun heisst es: such'!

WALTHER

Fräulein, verzeiht der Sitte Bruch.
Eines zu wissen, Eines zu fragen,
was müsst' ich nicht zu brechen wagen?

Ob Leben oder Tod? Ob Segen oder Fluch?
Mit einem Worte sei mir's vertraut:
mein Fräulein, sagt . . .

MAGDALENE *(zurückkommend)*

Hier ist das Tuch.

EVA

O weh! die Spange.

MAGDALENE

Fiel sie wohl ab?
(Sie geht abermals zurück.)

WALTHER

Ob Licht und Lust, oder Nacht und Grab?
Ob ich erfahr', wonach ich verlange,
ob ich vernehme, wovor mir graut:
Mein Fräulein, sagt . . .

MAGDALENE
(wieder zurückkommend)

Da ist auch die Spange.
Komm', Kind! Nun hast du Spang' und Tuch.
O weh! da vergass ich selbst mein Buch!
(Geht nochmals eilig nach hinten.)

WALTHER

Dies eine Wort, ihr sagt mir's nicht?
Die Silbe, die mein Urteil spricht?
Ja, oder nein!—ein flücht'ger Laut:
Mein Fräulein, sagt, seid ihr schon Braut?

MAGDALENE *(zu Walther)*

Sieh da, Herr Ritter,
wie sind wir hochgeehrt:
mit Evchen's Schutze
habt ihr euch gar beschwert?
Darf den Besuch des Helden
ich Meister Pogner melden?

WALTHER

O, betrat ich doch nie sein Haus!

DIE MEISTERSINGER VON NÜRNBERG

ACT ONE

The stage represents an oblique view of the church of St. Katharine; the last few rows of seats of the nave, which is on the left stretching toward the back, are visible: in front is the open space of the choir which is later shut off from the nave by a black curtain.

In the last row of seats Eva and Magdalene sit; Walther von Stolzing stands at some distance at the side leaning against a column with his eyes fixed on Eva, who frequently turns round towards him with mute gestures.

THE CONGREGATION

When to Thee our Saviour came
To be baptized in Thy name,
On the cross His life he gave,
So that we our souls might save;
Teaching us the Holy creed,
To be worthy of His deed.
Great Immerser,
Christ's Precursor!
Take us by Thy hand,
There on Jordan's strand!

(The congregation rises. All turn to the door and gradually leave the church during the voluntary. Walther fixes his gaze in great anxiety on Eva, who leaves her place at the same time and, followed by Magdalene, comes slowly towards him.)

WALTHER

Please wait! A word! Don't be unkind!

EVA *(to Magdalene)*

My kerchief! Look! It's left behind.

MAGDALENE

Forgetful child! I'll go and see.

WALTHER

Fräulein, I know it's bold of me,
yet I must ask you, do not deny me,
though every single rule defy me.

Your word means life or death, means
blessing or despair.
One word in answer before we part:
I beg you, tell . . .

MAGDALENE *(returning)*

It was right there.

EVA

O dear! My earring!

MAGDALENE

Did it fall off?
(She goes again to the back.)

WALTHER

Be it light and life, be it night and
death,
whether you say what I would like
hearing,
whether you put a knife in my heart,
I beg you, tell . . .

MAGDALENE *(returning again)*

I have found your earring.
Come, child, in future do take care.
Oh, dear! Now I left my prayer book
there!
(She goes off again hastily.)

WALTHER

A single word you can't deny,
that word will make me live or die,
yes or no, though it may smart,
please tell me if you've pledged your
heart!

MAGDALENE *(to Walther)*

My, my, what honor!
You have been more than kind;
to act as escort
I hope you did not mind.
Tell me, may master Pogner hear
that you have paid a visit here?

WALTHER

How I wish I had stayed away!

1

MAGDALENE

Ei! Junker! Was sagt ihr da aus?
In Nürnberg eben nur angekommen,
war't ihr nicht freundlich aufgenom-
men?
Was Küch' und Keller, Schrein und
Schrank
euch bot, verdient' es keinen Dank?

EVA

Gut Lenchen! Ach! das meint er ja
nicht.
Doch von mir wohl wünscht er Bericht.
Wie sag' ich's schnell? Versteh' ich's
doch kaum!
Mir ist, als wär' ich gar wie im Traum!
Er frägt, ob ich schon Braut.

MAGDALENE (heftig erschrocken)

Hilf Gott! Sprich nicht so laut!
Jetzt lass' uns nach Hause geh'n,
wenn uns die Leut' hier seh'n!

WALTHER

Nicht eh'r, bis ich alles weiss!

EVA (zu Magdalene)

'S ist leer, die Leut' sind fort.

MAGDALENE

D'rum eben wird mir heiss!
Herr Ritter, an and'rem Ort!
(David tritt aus der Sakristei ein, und
macht sich darüber her, die schwarzen Vorhänge zu schliessen.)

WALTHER (dringend)

Nein! Erst dies Wort!

EVA (zu Magdalene)

Dies Wort?

MAGDALENE

David? Ei! David hier?

EVA (zu Magdalene)

Was sag' ich? Sag' du's mir!

MAGDALENE

Herr Ritter, was ihr die Junger fragt,
das ist so leichtlich nicht gesagt.
Fürwahr ist Evchen Pogner Braut . . .

EVA

Doch hat noch keiner den Bräut'gam
erschaut.

MAGDALENE

Den Bräut'gam wohl noch niemand
kennt,
bis morgen ihn das Gericht ernennt,
das dem Meistersinger erteilt den Preis.

EVA (enthusiastisch)

Und selbst die Braut ihm reicht das
Reis.

WALTHER (verwundert)

Dem Meistersinger?

EVA (bang)

Seid ihr das nicht?

WALTHER

Ein Werbgesang?

MAGDALENE

Vor Wettgericht.

WALTHER

Den Preis gewinnt?

MAGDALENE

Wen die Meister meinen.

WALTHER

Die Braut dann wählt?

EVA (sich vergessend)

Euch oder keinen!

MAGDALENE

Was, Evchen! Evchen! Bist du von Sinnen?

EVA

Gut' Lene, hilf mir den Ritter gewinnen!

MAGDALENE

Sah'st ihn doch gestern zum ersten
Mal!

EVA

Das eben schuf mir so schnelle Qual,
dass ich schon längst ihn im Bilde sah!
Sag', trat er nicht ganz wie David
nah'?

MAGDALENE

Bist du toll? Wie David?

EVA

Wie David im Bild.

MAGDALENE

Ach! meinst du den König mit der Har-
fen
und langem Bart in der Meister Schild?

EVA

Nein, der, dess' Kiesel den Goliath war-
fen,
das Schwert im Gurt, die Schleuder zur
Hand,
das Haupt von lichten Locken um-
strahlt,
wie ihn uns Meister Dürer gemalt.

MAGDALENE

Good Lord, do you know what you say?
In Nürnberg where you arrived but
    newly,
were you not treated bountifully?
If stove and cellar offered you
their treats, then surely thanks are due.

EVA

Dear Lenchen, I'm afraid you don't
    see.
He is speaking only of me.
What can I say? How lost I must seem.
I feel as if I were in a dream.
He asks . . . about my heart!

MAGDALENE

Good God! Don't make me start!
Come, we must go home, my dear!
Someone might see us here!

WALTHER

But not till you let me know!

EVA (*to Magdalene*)

They're gone, there's no one here.

MAGDALENE

Exactly! Let us go.
The answer must be deferred.
(*David enters from the sacristy and
busies himself with closing the black
curtains.*)

WALTHER (*urgently*)

No! First that word!

EVA

That word!

MADALENE (*sees David*)

David? Why, David here?

EVA (*to Magdalene*)

I cannot . . . won't you, dear?

MAGDALENE

To answer what you have dared to ask
is surely not an easy task.
To someone she has pledged her heart.

EVA (*enthusiastically*)

But no one knows who'll be cast in
    the part!

MAGDALENE

It's true that no one knows his name
until the judges pronounce his fame
as a Mastersinger of true renown.

EVA

His bride will adorn his head with a
    crown.

WALTHER (*surprised*)

A Mastersinger?

EVA (*anxiously*)

Are you not one?

WALTHER

A courting song?

MAGDALENE

Where masters judge . . .

WALTHER

Who wins the prize?

MAGDALENE

Whom the masters favor.

WALTHER

The girl will choose . . . ?

EVA (*forgetting herself*)

You! or else no one!

MAGDALENE

But Evchen, Evchen, you must be rav-
    ing!

EVA

Good Lene, help me to win what I'm
    craving!

MAGDALENE

Yet you have seen him but once
    fore!

EVA

Yes, but it tortures me all the more
that I have seen him some other place!
I . . . thought I was seeing David's face.

MAGDALENE

Are you mad? Not David?

EVA

Yes, David in paint.

MAGDALENE

Ah, you mean the king with harp and
    flowing beard,
The Mastersingers' patron saint?

EVA

No! Him who once threw a stone at
    Goliath,
a sword he bears, a sling in his hand.
Around his head golden curls seem to
    shine,
as seen in master Dürer's design.

MAGDALENE (*laut seufzend*)
Ach, David! David!

DAVID
(*ein Lineal im Gürtel und ein grosses
Stück weisser Kreide an einer Schnur
schwenkend*)
Da bin ich! Wer ruft?

MAGDALENE
Ach, David! Was ihr für Unglück
schuft!
Der liebe Schelm! Wüsst' er's noch
nicht?
Ei, seht! da hat er uns gar verschlossen?

DAVID (*zärtlich*)
In's Herz euch allein!

MAGDALENE
Das treue Gesicht!
Ei, sagt! Was treibt ihr für Possen?

DAVID
Behüt es, Possen? Gar ernste Ding:
Für die Meister hier richt' ich den
Ring.

MAGDALENE
Wie? Gäb' es ein Singen?

DAVID
Nur Freiung heut':
der Lehrling wird da losgesprochen,
der nichts wider die Tabulatur ver-
brochen;
Meister wird, wen die Prob' nicht reut.

MAGDALENE
Da wär' der Ritter ja am rechten Ort.
Jetzt, Evchen, komm! Wir müssen fort.

WALTHER
Zu Meister Pogner lasst mich euch geleiten.

MAGDALENE
Erwartet den hier, er ist bald da.
Wollt ihr Evchen's Hand erstreiten,
rückt Ort und Zeit das Glück euch nah.

(*Zwei Lehrbuben tragen Bänke
herbei.*)

Jetzt eilig von hinnen!

WALTHER
Was soll ich beginnen?

MAGDALENE
Lasst David euch lehren,
die Freiung begehren.
Davidchen, hör', mein lieber Gesell':
den Ritter hier bewahr' mir wohl zur
Stell'!
Was Fein's aus der Küch'
bewahr' ich für dich,
und morgen begehr' du noch dreister,
wird hier der Junker heut' Meister!

EVA (*zu Walther*)
Seh' ich euch wieder?

WALTHER
Heut' Abend gewiss!
Was ich will wagen,
wie könnt' ich's sagen?
Neu ist mein Herz, neu mein Sinn!
Neu ist mir Alles, was ich beginn!
Eines nur weiss ich,
eines begreif' ich:
mit allen Sinnen
euch zu gewinnen!
Ist's mit dem Schwert nicht, muss es
gelingen,
gilt es als Meister euch zu ersingen.
Für euch Gut und Blut!
Für euch Dichter's heil'ger Mut!
Mein Herz, sel'ger Glut,
für euch liebesheil'ge Hut!

EVA
Mein Herz, sel'ger Glut, für euch
liebesheil'ge Hut.

MAGDALENE
Schnell heim! Sonst geht's nicht gut!
(*Sie zieht Eva rasch durch die Vor-
hänge fort.*)

DAVID
Gleich Meister? Oho! viel Mut!
(*Noch mehrere Lehrbuben sind einge-
treten, sie tragen und stellen Bänke,
und richten Alles zur Sitzung der
Meistersinger her.*)

ZWEITER LEHRBUBE
David, was stehst?

ERSTER LEHRBUBE
Greif' an's Werk!

ZWEITER LEHRBUBE
Hilf uns richten das Gemerk!

DAVID
Zu eifrigst war ich vor euch allen;
schafft nun für euch; hab' ander Gefallen!

MAGDALENE (*sighing aloud*)

Ah, David, David!

DAVID

(*returns, with a rule in his belt and a large piece of white chalk swinging by a string*)

I'm coming. Who calls?

MAGDALENE

Ah, David, how you have played us false!

(The little rogue, cause of my sighs!)

It seems you've locked up to make us stay here.

DAVID (*tenderly*)

You're locked in my heart!

MAGDALENE

How kind are his eyes!

Speak up! What game is this you play here?

DAVID

Beg pardon? Playing? A serious thing!

For the masters I must set the ring.

MAGDALENE

What? Someone is singing?

DAVID

Beginner's test; apprentices may win approbation

if they carefully follow each regulation.

Master is he who's deemed the best.

MAGDALENE

Then he can learn here what he wants to learn.

Now, Evchen, come, we must return.

WALTHER

To master Pogner's door I'll walk beside you.

MAGDALENE

Be patient and wait, he'll soon be here.

If she's not to be denied you,

then time and place for your luck are near.

But we must be going.

(*Two Prentices enter, carrying benches.*)

WALTHER

But what's to be done now?

MAGDALENE

Hear David's explanation

about your application.

David, be good, and do as I say:

this stranger here, be kind to him today.

Some goodies and some meat

I'll keep for you to eat,

your courting will be so much faster,

if he today is made a master!

EVA (*to Walther*)

When shall I see you?

WALTHER

Tonight without fail.

All my endeavor

is yours forever.

New is my thought, new my heart!

New every venture that I may start.

One thing I know now,

one thing is certain:

With every fiber

I will strive to win you!

If I can't do it with sword a-swinging

then as a master I'll win you singing.

For you soars my song,

a poet's love is holy and strong!

EVA

My love will be strong,

to you forever I'll belong.

MAGDALENE

Come home! Let's go! Things may go wrong!

Do come along!

(*She hurriedly pulls Eva away through the curtains.*)

DAVID

A master? He must be strong!

(*More Prentices have entered, they bring benches and place them in position, preparing everything for the meeting of the Mastersingers.*)

2ND PRENTICE

David! Come on!

1ST PRENTICE

Go to work!

2ND PRENTICE

Come and help us, do not shirk!

DAVID

You cannot accuse me of shirking:

do it yourself, I don't feel like working.

LEHRBUBEN

Was der sich dünkt!
Der Lehrling Muster!
Das macht, weil sein Meister ein Schus-
ter.
Beim Leisten sitzt er mit der Feder.
Beim dichten mit Draht und Pfriem'.
Sein' Verse schreibt er auf rohes Leder.
Das, dächt' ich, gerbten wir ihm!

DAVID

"Fanget an!"

WALTHER

Was soll's?

DAVID

"Fanget an!" So ruft der Merker:
nun sollt ihr singen! Wisst ihr das nicht?

WALTHER

Wer ist der Merker?

DAVID

Wisst ihr das nicht?
War't ihr noch nie bei'nem Sing-
gericht?

WALTHER

Noch nie, wo die Richter Handwerker.

DAVID

Seid ihr ein "Dichter?"

WALTHER

Wär ich's doch!

DAVID

Waret ihr "'Singer?"

WALTHER

Wüsst' ich's noch?

DAVID

Doch "Schulfreund" war't ihr, und
"Schüler" zuvor?

WALTHER

Das klingt mir alles fremd vor'm Ohr.

DAVID

Und so grad'hin wollt ihr Meister
werden?

WALTHER

Wie machte das so grosse Beschwerden?

DAVID

O Lene! Lene!

WALTHER

Wie ihr doch tut!

DAVID

O Magdalene!

WALTHER

Ratet mir gut!

DAVID (*setzt sich in Positur*)

Mein Herr! Der Singer Meisterschlag
gewinnt sich nicht in einem Tag.
In Nüremberg der grösste Meister,
mich lehrt die Kunst Hans Sachs;
schon voll ein Jahr mich unterweis't er,
dass ich als Schüler wachs'.
Schuhmacherei und Poeterei,
die lern' ich da all-einerlei:
hab' ich das Leder glatt geschlagen,
lern' ich Vokal and Konsonant sagen;
wichst' ich den Draht erst fest und steif,
was sich da reimt, ich wohl begreif'.
Den Pfriemen schwingend,
im Stich die Ahl',
was stumpf, was klingend,
was Mass und Zahl,
den Leisten im Schurz,
was lang, was kurz,
was hart, was lind,
hell oder blind,
was Waisen, was Milben,
was Kleb-Silben,
was Pausen, was Körner,
was Blumen, was Dörner,
das alles lernt' ich mit Sorg' und Acht:
wie weit nun, meint ihr, dass ich's gebracht?

WALTHER

Wohl zu 'nem Paar recht guter Schuh'?

DAVID

Ja, dahin hat's noch gute Ruh!
Ein "Bar" hat manch' Gesätz' und Gebänd';
wer da gleich die rechte Regel fänd',
die richt'ge Naht,
und den rechten Draht,
mit gutgefügten "Stollen,"
den Bar recht zu versohlen!
Und dann erst kommt der "Abgesang,"
das der nicht kurz, und nicht zu lang,
und auch keinen Reim enthält,
der schon im Stollen gestellt.
Wer alles das merkt, weiss und kennt,
wird doch immer noch nicht Meister
genennt.

PRENTICES

He's full of beans!
The Prentice's model!
He thinks he has learned how to cobble!
He makes his shoes with quill and feather!
His poems with awl and pin!
His verse is written on untanned leather.
Let's start, then, tanning his skin.

DAVID

"Now begin!"

WALTHER

What's that?

DAVID

"Now begin!" So cries the marker,
that means start singing! Have you not guessed?

WALTHER

Who is the marker?

DAVID

Haven't you guessed?
Haven't you been to a singing test?

WALTHER

But not where the judges were craftsmen.

DAVID

Are you a "Poet"?

WALTHER

Were it so!

DAVID

Are you a "Singer"?

WALTHER

I don't know.

DAVID

A "Pupil"? "Friend of the School" you must be!

WALTHER

All that sounds very strange to me.

DAVID

And you want to be a master without it?

WALTHER

Why, what is all the trouble about it?

DAVID

O Lene! Lene!

WALTHER

Don't carry on!

DAVID

O Magdalene!

WALTHER

What's to be done?

DAVID

You see! The master's lofty height
cannot be scaled from morn to night.
The great Hans Sachs has been my master:
he taught me all he knew!
And yet a year meanwhile has passed ere
I as a student grew.
How to make shoes and verses that rhyme
I'm trying to learn all the time.
Once with the leather I've done my duty,
then I learn vowel and consonant beauty;
once I have drawn and waxed a wire,
then to a rhyme I may aspire.
My bodkin swinging,
my awl I clutch,
what's bleak, what's ringing,
what's little, what's much,
I test with my last
what's slow, what's fast,
what's dull, what's shined;
sparkling or blind,
or orphans or patches
or wordsnatches,
or pauses or trickles
or flowers and prickles,
In all these things I was trained and briefed.
How much, I ask you, have I achieved?

WALTHER

I'd say a pair of solid shoes?

DAVID

If you were right, that would be news.
A verse is built according to rules,
you must use them as you use your tools.
You make a stitch,
then you put on pitch.
The verses need resoling,
the stanzas overhauling.
And then make sure the after-song
is not too short and not too long;
and it must not use any more
rhymes that were heard once before.
When all this you know bar by bar,
then they still won't call you master by far.

WALTHER

Hilf Gott! Will ich denn Schuster sein?
In die Singkunst lieber führ' mich ein.

DAVID

Ja, hätt ich's nur selbst erst zum Singer gebracht!
Wer glaubt wohl, was das für Mühe
macht!
Der Meister Tön' und Weisen,
gar viel an Nam' und Zahl,
die starken und die leisen,
wer die wüsste allzumal!
Der kurze, lang' and überlang' Ton,
die Schreibpapier, Schwarztintenweis';
der rote, blau' und grüne Ton;
die Hageblüh', Strohhalm, Fengelweis';
der zarte, der süsse, der Rosenton;
der kurzen Liebe, der vergess'ne Ton;
die Rosmarin, Gelbveigleinweis',
die Regenbogen, die Nachtigallweis';
die englische Zinn, die Zimmtröhren-
weis';
frisch Pomeranzen, grün' Lindenblüh
weis';
die Frösch, die Kälber, die Stieglitzweis',
die abgeschied'ne Vielfrassweis',
der Lerchen, der Schnecken, der Beller-
ton;
die Melissenblümlein, die Meiranweis',
gelb Löwenhaut, treu Pelikanweis',
die butterglänzende Drahtweis'!

WALTHER

Hilf Himmel! Welch' endlos' Tönege-
leis!

DAVID

Das sind nur die Namen: nun lernt sie
singen,
recht wie die Meister sie gestellt.
Jed' Wort und Ton muss klärlich
klingen,
wo steigt die Stimm' und wo sie fällt;
fangt nicht zu hoch, zu tief nicht an,
als es die Stimm' erreichen kann.
Mit dem Atem spart, dass er nicht
knappt
und gar am End' ihr überschnappt;
vor dem Wort mit der Stimme ja nicht
summt,
nach dem Wort mit dem Mund auch
nicht brummt.
Nicht ändert an Blum' und Koloratur,
jed' Zierrat fest nach des Meisters Spur.

Verwechseltet ihr, würdet gar irr,
verlört ihr euch und käm't ins Gewirr;
wär' sonst euch alles auch gelungen,
da hättet ihr gar versungen.
Trotz grossem Fleiss und Emsigkeit,
ich selbst noch bracht' es nicht so weit:
so oft ich's versucht' und's nicht gelingt,
die Knieriemschlagweis' der Meister
mir singt.
Wenn dann Jungfer Lene nicht Hilfe
weiss,
sing ich die eitel Brot und Wasserweis!
Nehmt euch ein Beispiel d'ran,
und lasst vom Meisterwahn!
Denn "Singer" und "Dichter" müsst Ihr
sein,
eh' ihr zum Meister kehret ein.

LEHRBUBEN

David!

WALTHER

Wer ist nun "Dichter"?

LEHRBUBEN

David! kommst her?

DAVID

Wartet nur—gleich! Wer Dichter wär?
Habt ihr zum Singer euch aufgeschwun-
gen,
und der Meister Töne richtig gesungen,
fügtet ihr selbst nun Reim' und Wort',
dass sie genau an Stell' und Ort
passten zu einem Meisterton,
dann trügt ihr den Dichterpreis davon.

LEHRBUBEN

He! David! Soll man's dem Meister
klagen?
Wirst' dich bald deines Schwatzens
entschlagen?

DAVID

Oho! Ja wohl! Denn helf' ich euch
nicht,
ohne mich wird alles doch falsch
gericht'!

WALTHER

Nur dies noch: wer wird Meister
genannt?

DAVID

Damit, Herr Ritter, ist's so bewandt:
Der Dichter, der aus eig'nem Fleisse,
zu Wort' und Reimen, die er erfand,
aus Tönen auch fügt eine neue Weise;
der wird als "Meistersinger" erkannt.

WALTHER

Good Lord! Who wants to make a shoe?
As a singer what has one to do?

DAVID

Well, I tried to be one, but didn't
succeed!
It's frightening, what patience singers
need!
The masters' tunes and meters
are all too many to recall.
The bitter and the sweeter,
lucky man who knows them all!
The shorter, long and overlong tone,
the parchment air, blacktinted air;
the reddish blue and greenish tone;
the hawthorn air, strawblade, fennel
air;
the tender, the sweetest, the rosebud
tone;
of fleeting passion, the forsaken tone;
the mignonette, wallflower air,
the rainbow iris, the nightingale air,
the angel's height, the cinnamon air,
fresh pomegranate, green lindenblossom
air;
the frog, the oxen, the goldfinch air;
the hibernating glutton air,
the skylark, the tortoise, the barker's
tone,
and the balmmint flower, the mar-
joram air,
brown lionskin, true pelican air,
the bright shining wire air!

WALTHER

God help me! Those airs will drive me
to despair!

DAVID

Those were but the names, though.
Now to the singing;
like every master of renown
each word and tune you must set
ringing,
the voice ascends and then comes
down.
Don't start too high, don't start too low
and thus find out how far you can go.
Do not waste your breath; that's a mistake;
before you've done, your voice would
break.
And before you begin, don't ever hum;
at the end, keep your mouth closed and
mum.
Don't change any trill, or colorature;
each grace note follows the masters'
trace.

If you get confused, in any way,
if you get lost, or led astray:
however good was your beginning,
you'll not stand a chance of winning!
It matters not how hard I toiled,
my efforts so far have been foiled.
Whenever I tried, and ended in defeat,
the "knee-belt-hit" tune my master
would beat.
And were't not for Lene, so kind, so
fair,
I'd have to sing the "Bread and Water"
air!
Your case might be the same,
give up your master claim!
As singer and poet you must be famed
ere as a master you're acclaimed!

PRENTICES

David!

WALTHER

Whom do you call poet?

PRENTICES

David! Come here!

DAVID

Wait a bit. Wait! The poet's task?
If as a singer you are admired,
and the master's airs have duly
acquired,
then if you write your own word and
rhyme,
making them fit in place and time,
neatly, another master's tune:
then you'll be a poet very soon!

PRENTICES

Hey! David! Shall we inform your
master?
Then you'll stop all that chatter much
faster!

DAVID

Oho! For sure! If I'm not along,
what you try without me is always
wrong!

WALTHER

One more thing: who's called master,
I ask?

DAVID

To earn that title is quite a task.
A poet who, through inspiration,
to fit the words and rhymes he found,
composes a tune of his own creation,
will be as Mastersinger renowned.

WALTHER (*rasch*)

So bleibt mir einzig der Meisterlohn!
Muss ich singen,
kann's nur gelingen,
find' ich zum Vers auch den eig'nen
Ton.

DAVID

(*der sich zu den Lehrbuben gewendet
hat*)

Was macht ihr denn da? Ja, fehl' ich
beim Werk,
verkehrt nur richtet ihr Stuhl und Gemerk!
Ist denn heut' Singschul? Dass ihr's
wisst,
das kleine Gemerk! Nur "Freiung" ist!

DIE LEHRBUBEN

Aller End' ist doch David der Allerge-
scheit'st'!
Nach hohen Ehren gewiss er geizt:
's ist Freiung heut';
gewiss er freit,
als vornehmer Singer er schon sich
spreizt!
Die Schlagreime fest er inne hat,
Arm-Hunger-Weise singt er glatt;
Doch die Harte-Tritt-Weis', die kennt
er am best',
die trat ihm sein Meister hart und fest!

DAVID

Ja, lacht nur zu! Heut' bin ich's nicht.
Ein Andrer stellt sich zum Gericht:
der war nicht Schüler, ist nicht Singer,
den Dichter, sagt er, überspring' er;
denn er ist Junker,
und mit einem Sprung er
denkt ohne weit're Beschwerden
heut' hier Meister zu werden.
D'rum richtet nur fein
das Gemerk dem ein!
Dorthin! Hierher die Tafel an die
Wand,
so dass sie recht dem Merker zur Hand!
Ja, ja, dem Merker! Wird euch wohl
bang?
Vor ihm schon mancher Werber
versang.
Sieben Fehler gibt er euch vor,
die merkt er mit Kreide dort an;
wer über sieben Fehler verlor
hat versungen und ganz vertan!
Nun nehmt euch in Acht.
Der Merker wacht.
Glück auf zum Meistersingen!
Mögt' euch das Kränzlein erschwingen!

Das Blumenkränzlein aus Seiden fein,
wird das dem Herrn Ritter beschieden
sein?

DIE LEHRBUBEN

(*welche das Gemerk zugleich geschlossen, fassen sich an und tanzen einen
verschlungenen Reihen darum*)

Das Blumenkränzlein aus Seiden fein,
wird das dem Herrn Ritter beschieden
sein?

(*Walther, verdriesslich über das Gespött
der Knaben, hat sich auf die vordere
Bank niedergelassen. Pogner ist mit
Beckmesser im Gespräch aus der Sakristei aufgetreten. Die Lehrbuben
harren ehrerbietig vor der hintern
Bank stehend. Nur David stellt sich
anfänglich am Eingang der Sakristei
auf.*)

POGNER (*zu Beckmesser*)

Seid meiner Treue wohl versehen;
was ich bestimmt, ist euch zu Nutz:
im Wettgesang müsst ihr bestehen,
wer böte euch als Meister Trutz?

BECKMESSER

Doch wollt ihr von dem Punkt nicht
weichen,
der mich—ich sag's—bedenklich
macht:
kann Evchen's Wunsch den Werber
streichen,
was nützt mir meine Meisterpracht?

POGNER

Ei sagt! Ich mein', vor allen Dingen
sollt' euch an dem gelegen sein?
Könnt ihr der Tochter Wunsch nicht
zwingen,
wie möchtet ihr wohl um sie frei'n?

BECKMESSER

Ei ja! Gar wohl! D'rum eben bitt' ich,
dass bei dem Kind ihr für mich sprecht,
wie ich geworben zart und sittig,
und wie Beckmesser grad' euch recht.

POGNER

Das tu' ich gern.

BECKMESSER (*bei Seite*)

Er lässt nicht nach!
Wie wehrt' ich da 'nem Ungemach?

WALTHER (*zu Pogner*)

Gestattet, Meister!

POGNER

Wie mein Junker?
Ihr sucht mich in der Singschul' hier?

WALTHER

Then I must conquer the master
     throne!
As a singer
I'll be the winner,
finding for my verse also a tune of my
     own!

DAVID (*to the Prentices*)

What dunces you are! And that is the
     truth.
You don't know where to put stool and
     booth!
This is not a schoolday. I know best!
The little booth today! A singing test!

PRENTICES

Don't you find our David's the smart-
     est of all?
He's so ambitious, he's riding for a fall.
A singing test; he, too, will sing.
An excellent singer is waiting for his
     call!
The hard-hitting rhymes are in his
     throat.
The hunger tune he learned by rote,
but a black and blue kick air he knows
     beat by beat;
his master engraved it on his seat!

DAVID

Yes, laugh away! But not at me.
Another candidate you will see.
He is no singer, was no pupil;
The poet he waives without a scruple;
he's so superior
that he has no fear or
doubt that his luck will ever fail him,
or that as master we'll hail him.
Now come set the stage
for the marker's cage.
This way! That way! The blackboard
     on the stool;
the marker uses this as his tool.
I said: The Marker! Maybe you
     quailed?
Because of him many candidates failed.
Seven errors don't count in the score;
he marks them with chalk on his slate.
But if you make but one error more,
as a singer you've sealed your fate!
You'd better beware:
the marker's there!
Now here's to a glad beginning!
Here's hoping you will be winning.

The flower chaplet with silken trim;
we wonder if that will be given to him.
(*The Prentices, who have completed
the marker's booth, join hands and
dance in a ring around it.*)

PRENTICES

The flower chaplet with silken trim,
we wonder if that will be given to him!
(*Walther, vexed with the boys' mocking, has seated himself on the front
bench. Pogner has come from the
sacristy in conversation with Beckmesser. The Prentices stand waiting
respectfully before the back bench.
Only David takes his place at first
by the sacristy door.*)

POGNER (*to Beckmesser*)

I can assure you I am loyal;
what I've decreed will serve your aim
But first you fight the battle royal,
you're sure to win the master game.

BECKMESSER

But won't you waive the one condition
at which, I fear, I boggle still.
If Evchen makes her own decision,
what good is all my master skill?

POGNER

Against her wish I can't protect you;
My child is free to choose her life.
But if my daughter should reject you,
you'd hardly want her for your wife?

BECKMESSER

Indeed! That's true. That's why I'm
     saying:
defend my cause as best you can;
speak of the court I have been paying;
say that Beckmesser is your man.

POGNER

You have my word.

BECKMESSER (*aside*)

He won't give way.
How will I then avoid dismay?

WALTHER (*to Pogner*)

Allow me, master!

POGNER

Walther Stolzing!
What brought you to this church to-
     day?

BECKMESSER (*bei Seite*)
Verstünden's die Frau'n! Doch
  schlechtes Geflunker
gilt ihnen mehr als all' Poesie.

WALTHER
Hie eben bin ich am rechten Ort.
Gesteh' ich's frei, vom Lande fort
was mich nach Nürnberg trieb,
war nur zur Kunst die Lieb'.
Vergass ich's gestern euch zu sagen,
heut' muss ich's laut zu künden wagen:
ein Meistersinger möcht' ich sein.
Schliesst, Meister, in die Zunft mich ein.

POGNER
Kunz Vogelgesang! Freund Nachtigall
Hört doch, welch ganz besondrer Fall!
Der Ritter hier, mir wohlbekannt,
hat der Meisterkunst sich zugewandt.

BECKMESSER
Noch such' ich's zu wenden: doch sollt's
  nicht gelingen;
versuch ich des Mädchens Herz zu ersingen;
in stiller Nacht, von ihr nur gehört,
erfahr' ich, ob auf mein Lied sie
  schwört.
    (*Walther erblickend*)
Wer ist der Mensch?

POGNER (*zu Walther*)
Glaubt, wie mich's freut!
Die alte Zeit dünkt mich erneut.

BECKMESSER
Er gefällt mir nicht!

POGNER
Was ihr begehrt,
soviel an mir sei's euch gewährt.

BECKMESSER
Was will der hier? Wie der Blick ihm
  lacht!

POGNER
Half ich euch gern bei Gut's Verkauf,
in die Zunft nun nehm' ich euch
  gleich gern auf.

BECKMESSER
Holla Sixtus! Auf den hab' Acht!

WALTHER
Habt Dank der Güte
aus tiefstem Gemüte!
Und darf ich denn hoffen,
steht heut' mir noch offen,
zu werben um den Preis,
dass Meistersinger ich heiss'?

BECKMESSER
Oho! Fein sacht! Auf dem Kopf steht
  kein Kegel!

POGNER
Herr Ritter, dies geh' nun nach der
  Regel.
Doch heut' ist Freiung, ich schlag' euch
  vor,
mir leihen die Meister ein willig Ohr.
(*Die Meistersinger sind nun alle ange-
langt, zuletzt auch Hans Sachs.*)

SACHS
Gott grüss' euch, Meister!

VOGELGESANG
Sind wir beisammen?

BECKMESSER
Der Sachs is ja da!

NACHTIGALL
So ruft die Namen!

KOTHNER
(*zieht eine Liste hervor*)
Zu einer Freiung und Zunftberatung
ging an die Meister ein' Einladung:
bei Nenn' und Nam',
ob jeder kam,
ruf' ich nun auf, als letzt-entbot'ner,
der ich mich nenn' und bin Fritz
  Kothner.
Seit ihr da, Veit Pogner?

POGNER
Hier zur Hand.

KOTHNER
Kunz Vogelgesang?

VOGELGESANG
Ein sich fand.

KOTHNER
Hermann Ortel?

ORTEL
Immer am Ort.

KOTHNER
Balthasar Zorn?

ZORN
Bleibt niemals fort.

KOTHNER
Konrad Nachtigall?

NACHTIGALL
Treu seinem Schlag.

BECKMESSER (*aside*)

If women but knew! What sounds high
   falutin'
women prefer to what is sublime!

WALTHER

This place is fitting, it would appear;
let me be frank: what brought me here,
what made me leave my hearth
was only love for art.
Last night, it's true, I failed to mention,
but now I tell you my intention:
a mastersinger I want to be.
Please open your guild to me!

POGNER (*to some of the Masters*)

Kunz Vogelgesang! Friend Nachtigall!
This is the strangest case of all.
This noble man I've known so long
wants to give his life to master song.

BECKMESSER

Once more I must try it; but if he
   won't alter,
I'm sure when she hears me sing, her
   heart will falter;
when all's asleep but she and the moon,
I'll find out if she adores my tune.

(*seeing Walther*)

Who is that man?

POGNER (*to Walther*)

Glad that you came!
The good old times seem back again.

BECKMESSER

I don't like his looks!

POGNER

About your plan,
I'll do my best, depend on me.

BECKMESSER

What does he want? What a daring
   glance!

POGNER

Just as I helped you to sell your land,
I will gladly help you in your demand.

BECKMESSER

Look out, Sixtus! Don't take a chance!

WALTHER

The thanks I owe you
I promise to show you.
As hope springs forever,
I will yet endeavor
to fight for what I claimed
and Mastersinger be named.

BECKMESSER

I knew at once that his head must be
   hollow!

POGNER

Friend Walther: there are rules we
   have to follow,
but I'll propose you right now and here.
The masters will lend me a willing ear.

(*All the masters have now arrived,
   Hans Sachs last.*)

SACHS

God bless you, masters!

VOGELGESANG

Everyone in now?

BECKMESSER

Since Sachs has arrived!

NACHTIGALL

Then let's begin now!

KOTHNER (*produces a list*)

All the masters received invitations
for a contest and consultations.
Each single name,
to see who came,
I'll call as last invited voter.
Let it be known: I'm called Fritz
   Kothner.
Are you here, Veit Pogner?

POGNER

I am here.

KOTHNER

Kunz Vogelgesang?

VOGELGESANG

Did appear.

KOTHNER

Hermann Ortel?

ORTEL

Right on the spot.

KOTHNER

Balthasar Zorn?

ZORN

I'm on the dot.

KOTHNER

Konrad Nachtigall?

NACHTIGALL

True to his song.

KOTHNER

Augustin Moser?

MOSER

Nie fehlen mag.

KOTHNER

Niklaus Vogel? Schweigt?

EIN LEHRBUBE

Ist krank!

KOTHNER

Gut' Bess'rung dem Meister!

ALLE MEISTER

Walt's Gott!

DER LEHRBUBE

Schön Dank!

KOTHNER

Hans Sachs?

DAVID

Da steht er!

SACHS

Juckt dir das Fell?
Verzeiht, Meister! Sachs ist zur Stell'

KOTHNER

Sixtus Beckmesser?

BECKMESSER

Immer bei Sachs,
das den Reim ich lern' von "blüh und
    wachs."

KOTHNER

Ulrich Eisslinger?

EISSLINGER

Hier!

KOTHNER

Hans Foltz?

FOLTZ

Bin da.

KOTHNER

Hans Schwarz?

SCHWARZ

Zuletzt: Gott wollt's!

KOTHNER

Zur Sitzung gut und voll die Zahl.
Beliebt's, wir schreiten zur Merkerwahl?

VOGELGESANG

Wohl eh'r nach dem Fest?

BECKMESSER

Pressiert's den Herrn?
Mein' Stell' und Amt lass' ich ihm gern.

POGNER

Nicht doch, ihr Meister! Lasst das jetzt
    fort!
Für wicht'gen Antrag bitt' ich um's
    Wort.

KOTHNER

Das habt ihr; Meister, sprecht!

POGNER

Nun hört, und versteht mich recht!
Das schöne Fest, Johannistag,
ihr wisst, begeh'n wir morgen:
auf grüner Au', am Blumenhag,
bei Spiel und Tanz im Lustgelag,
an froher Brust geborgen,
vergessen seiner Sorgen,
ein Jeder freut sich, wie er mag.
Die Singschul' ernst im Kirchenchor
die Meister selbst vertauschen,
mit Kling und Klang hinaus zum Tor,
auf off'ne Wiese zieh'n sie vor,
bei hellen Festes Rauschen
das Volk sie lassen lauschen
dem Freigesang mit Laien Ohr.
Zu einem Werb' und Wettgesang
gestellt sind Siegespreise,
und beide preist man weit und lang,
die Gabe wie die Weise.
Nun schuf mich Gott zum reichen
    Mann;
und gibt ein Jeder, wie er kann,
so musste ich wohl sinnen,
was ich gäb' zu gewinnen,
dass ich nicht käm' zu Schand';
so hört denn, was ich fand.
In deutschen Landen viel gereist,
hat oft es mich verdrossen,
dass man den Bürger wenig preist,
ihn karg nennt und verschlossen.
An Höfen, wie an nied'rer Statt,
des bitt'ren Tadels ward ich satt,
dass nur auf Schacher und Geld,
sein Merk' der Bürger stellt.
Dass wir im weiten deutschen Reich
die Kunst einzig noch pflegen,
d'ran dünkt ihnen wenig gelegen.
Doch wie uns das zur Ehre gereich',
und dass mit hohem Mut
wir schätzen, was schön und gut,
was wert die Kunst, und was sie gilt,
das ward ich der Welt zu zeigen gewillt,
d'rum hört, Meister, die Gab',
die als Preis bestimmt ich hab'!
Dem Singer, der im Kunstgesang
vor allem Volk den Preis errang
am Sankt Johannistag,

KOTHNER

Augustin Moser?

MOSER

I've come along.

KOTHNER

Niklaus Vogel? Absent?

PRENTICE

He's ill!

KOTHNER

Please tell him we're sorry.

ALL MASTERS

We are!

PRENTICE

I will.

KOTHNER

Hans Sachs?

DAVID

He's present!

SACHS

You want to be tanned?
Forgive, masters! Sachs is at hand.

KOTHNER

Sixtus Beckmesser?

BECKMESSER

Always with Sachs,
So that I find a rhyme for "that's the
crux"!

KOTHNER

Ulrich Eisslinger?

EISSLINGER

Yes!

KOTHNER

Hans Foltz?

FOLTZ

I'm here.

KOTHNER

Hans Schwartz?

SCHWARTZ

I'm here! Let's start!

KOTHNER

It seems the quorum is complete.
Let's vote: who'll sit in the marker's
seat?

VOGELGESANG

Perhaps that can wait.

BECKMESSER

I get the hint.
Whoever cares may do my stint.

POGNER

Now please, no fighting, upon my
word!
I ask you, masters, may I be heard?

KOTHNER

Veit Pogner, yes you may!

POGNER

Now hear what I have to say.
That lovely day, Midsummer Day,
we celebrate tomorrow.
On verdant meadows, on every way,
with games and dancing, all will be
gay;
they'll come from every borough,
forgetting all their sorrow,
they'll be as merry as they may.
The guildschool, grave tradition bound,
which is the masters' station,
we'll leave tomorrow, and we'll be
found
with drum and fife, on open ground.
In festive jubilation,
the city's population
will listen to the masters' sound.
We offer for the tests we hold
awards of various sizes,
and far and wide they'll be extolled,
the singing and the prizes.
I am, thank God, a wealthy man.
And each one gives as best he can;
and so I've searched my coffer
for gifts that I may offer
to keep my honor sound,
and this is what I found:
wherever German land I tread,
I find with indignation,
we're rarely praised and have instead
a miser's reputation.
I've heard it from both high and low;
I'm sick of hearing wherever I go
that we have bargained and sold
our lives and souls for gold.
It's thanks to us that far and wide
our art is still respected,
but they think this can be neglected.
Yet, it's to us a cause for pride,
and that with all our heart
we treasure what's fine in art;
and how its every call we heed,
I've made up my mind to show with a
deed.
Now hear, masters, what I chose
as the prize that I propose.
The singer who in word and song
is judged the best before the throng,
on this Midsummer Day,

sei er, wer er auch mag,
dem geb' ich, ein Kunstgewog'ner,
von Nürenberg Veit Pogner,
mit all' meinem Gut, wie's geh' und
    steh',
Eva, mein einzig Kind, zur Eh'!

DIE MEISTER
(*sehr lebhaft durcheinander*)

Das heisst ein Wort! Ein Wort, ein
    Mann!
Da sieht man, was ein Nürnberger
    kann!
D'rob preist man euch noch weit und
    breit,
den wack'ren Bürger Pogner Veit!

DIE LEHRBUBEN (*lustig aufspringend*)

Alle Zeit, weit und breit:
Pogner Veit!

VOGELGESANG

Wer möchte da nicht ledig sein!

SACHS

Sein Weib gäb' mancher gern wohl
    d'rein!

KOTHNER

Auf, ledig' Mann!
Jetzt macht euch 'ran!

POGNER

Nun hört noch, wie ich's ernstlich
    mein'!
Ein' leblos' Gabe stell' ich nicht;
ein Mägdlein sitzt mit zum Gericht:
den Preis erkennt die Meisterzunft;
doch gilt's der Eh', so will's Vernunft,
dass ob der Meister Rat
die Braut den Ausschlag hat.

BECKMESSER (*zu Kothner*)

Dünkt euch das klug?

KOTHNER

Versteh' ich gut,
ihr gebt uns in des Mägdlein's Hut?

BECKMESSER

Gefährlich das!

KOTHNER

Stimmt es nicht bei,
wie wäre dann der Meister Urteil frei?

BECKMESSER

Lasst's gleich wählen nach Herzen's
    Ziel,
und lasst den Meistergesang aus dem
    Spiel!

POGNER

Nicht so! Wie doch? Versteht mich
    recht!
Wem ihr Meister den Preis zusprecht,
die Maid kann dem verwehren,
doch nie einen Andren begehren.
Ein Meistersinger muss er sein;
nur wen ihr krönt, den soll sie frei'n.

SACHS

Verzeiht! Vielleicht schon ginget ihr zu
    weit.
Ein Mädchenherz und Meisterkunst
erglüh'n nicht stets in gleicher Brunst:
der Frauen Sinn, gar unbelehrt,
dünkt mich dem Sinn des Volk's gleich
    wert.
Wollt ihr nun vor dem Volke zeigen,
wie hoch die Kunst ihr ehrt,
und lasst ihr dem Kind die Wahl zu
    eigen,
wollt nicht, dass dem Spruch es wehrt:
so lasst das Volk auch Richter sein,
mit dem Kinde sicher stimmt's überein.

DIE MEISTER

Oho! Das Volk? Ja, das wäre schön!
Ade dann Kunst und Meistertön'!

KOTHNER

Nein, Sachs! Gewiss, das hat keinen
    Sinn!
Gäb't ihr dem Volk die Regeln hin?

SACHS

Vernehmt mich recht! Wie ihr doch
    tut!
Gesteht, ich kenn' die Regeln gut,
und dass die Zunft die Regeln bewahr',
bemüh' ich mich selbst schon manches
    Jahr.
Doch einmal im Jahre fänd' ich's weise,
dass man die Regeln selbst probier',
ob in der Gewohnheit trägem G'leise
ihr' Kraft und Leben nicht sich verlier'!
Und ob ihr der Natur
noch seid auf rechter Spur,
das sagt euch nur,
wer nichts weiss von der Tabulatur.
(*Die Lehrbuben springen auf und
reiben sich die Hände.*)

BECKMESSER

Hei! wie sich die Buben freuen!

SACHS (*eifrig fortfahrend*)

D'rum mocht' es euch nie gereuen,
dass jährlich am Sankt Johannisfest,
statt dass das Volk man kommen lässt,
herab aus hoher Meisterwolk'

let him be who he may,
him I'll give an art's admirer
of Nürnberg, Veit Pogner,
along with the fruits of all my life,
Eva, my only child, as his wife!

THE MASTERS

(*rising and speaking to each other with
great animation*)

A manly word! As good as you!
And spoken like a Nürnberger, too!
That's why your fame is shining bright,
the valiant burgher, Pogner Veit!

PRENTICES (*springing up merrily*)

Shining bright! Day and night!
Pogner Veit!

VOGELGESANG

Not to be married one might be keen!

SACHS

Some wish that they had never been!

KOTHNER

Come, single man,
do what you can!

POGNER

Now, mind you, this is what I mean:
a lifeless gift I don't bestow;
my child may say a final "no!"
The masters' guild awards the prize;
as for the maid, it's only wise
that, once you've said your word,
her wishes should be heard.

BECKMESSER (*to Kothner*)

You think that's right?

KOTHNER

I understand;
you put us in your daughter's hand?

BECKMESSER

I smell a rat!

KOTHNER

If she can choose,
the judgment of the masters is no use.

BECKMESSER

Let her follow her loving heart,
and let's forget about masters and art!

POGNER

Not so! My friends, no need to frown.
To the man whom you masters crown
she may deny her favor,
but must stay a spinster forever.
A mastersinger he must be,
one whom you crown to wed she's free.

SACHS

May I? Perhaps you're aiming all too
high.
A maiden's heart, a master's aim,
don't always burn with equal flame.
A woman's thoughts, the people's mind,
they are alike, I think, in kind.
Now, if you want to show your neighbors
how much you treasure art,
and let her select the man she favors
and have all dissension barred,
then let the people raise their voice—
they'll agree with Evchen making her
choice!

THE MASTERS

Oho! What's that? Yes, that's all we
need.
Farewell to art and master creed!

KOTHNER

No Sachs, I'm sure, that makes little
sense,
putting the rules in the people's hands!

SACHS

Do hear me out! So much ado!
I know the rules as well as you.
To keep those rules from any slight
has been my endeavor day and night.
But once every year it might be clever
to put the rules themselves to a test,
whether, running in lazy custom forever,
their vital strength remains at its best.
And whether you betray
the law of nature's way,
who else can say
but those who have no laws to obey!
(*The Prentices jump up and rub their
hands.*)

BECKMESSER

Hey! Look how those rascals love it!

SACHS (*eagerly continuing*)

I'm sure it would be to your profit
if yearly on this Midsummer Day,
rather than make them come your way,
you'd climb down from your master
cloud,

ihr selbst euch wendet zu dem Volk.
Dem Volke wollt ihr behagen,
nun däcdt' ich, läg' es nah,
ihr liesst es selbst euch auch sagen,
ob das ihm zur Lust geschah.
Dass Volk und Kunst gleich blüh' und
wachs',
bestellt ihr so, mein' ich, Hans Sachs!

VOGELGESANG
Ihr meint's wohl recht!

KOTHNER
Doch steht's drum faul.

NACHTIGALL
Wenn spricht das Volk, halt' ich das
Maul.

KOTHNER
Der Kunst droht allweil Fall und
Schmach,
läuft sie der Gunst des Volkes nach.

BECKMESSER
D'rin bracht' er's weit, der hier so
dreist:
Gassenhauer dichtet er meist.

POGNER
Freund Sachs! Was ich mein', ist schon
neu;
zuviel auf einmal brächte Reu'!
So frag' ich, ob den Meistern gefällt
Gab' und Regel, so wie ich's gestellt?
(Die Meister erheben sich beistim-
mend.)

SACHS
Mir genügt der Jungfer Ausschlag-
stimm.

BECKMESSER
Der Schuster weckt doch stets mir
Grimm!

KOTHNER
Wer schreibt sich als Werber ein?
Ein Junggesell muss er sein!

BECKMESSER
Vielleicht auch ein Witwer? Fragt nur
den Sachs!

SACHS
Nicht doch, Herr Merker! Aus jüng'rem
Wachs
als ich und ihr muss der Freier sein,
soll Evchen ihm den Preis verleih'n.

BECKMESSER
Als wie auch ich? Grober Gesell!

KOTHNER
Begehrt wer Freiung, der komm' zur
Stell'!
Ist Jemand gemeld't, der Freiung
begehrt?

POGNER
Wohl, Meister zur Tagesordnung kehrt
und nehmt von mir Bericht,
wie ich auf Meisterpflicht
einen jungen Ritter empfehle,
der will, dass man ihn wähle,
und heut' als Meistersinger frei'.
Mein Junker Stolzing, kommt herbei!
(Walther tritt vor und verneigt sich.)

BECKMESSER (für sich)
Dacht' ich mir's doch! Geht's da hinaus,
Veit?

(laut)
Meister, ich mein', zu spät ist's der Zeit.

DIE MEISTER
Der Fall ist neu. Ein Ritter gar?
Soll man sich freu'n? Wäre da Gefahr?
Immerhin hat's ein gross' Gewicht,
dass Meister Pogner für ihn spricht.

KOTHNER
Soll uns der Junker willkommen sein,
zuvor muss er wohl vernommen sein.

POGNER
Vernehmt mich wohl! Wünsch' ich ihm
Glück,
nicht bleib' ich doch hinter der Regel
zurück.
Tut, Meister, die Fragen!

KOTHNER
So mög' uns der Junker sagen:
ist er frei und ehrlich geboren?

POGNER
Die Frage gebt verloren,
da ich euch selbst dess' Bürge steh',
dass er aus frei und edler Eh':
von Stolzing Walther aus Frankenland,
nach Brief und Urkund mir wohlbekannt.
Als seines Stammes letzter Spross,
verliess er neulich Hof und Schloss
und zog nach Nürnberg her,
dass er hier Bürger wär'.

BECKMESSER
Neu Junkerunkraut! Tut nicht gut.

NACHTIGALL
Freund Pogner's Wort Genüge tut.

SACHS
Wie längst von den Meistern beschlos-
sen ist,
ob Herr, ob Bauer, hier nichts
beschiesst:
hier fragt sich's nach der Kunst allein,
wer will ein Meistersinger sein.

address yourselves to all the crowd.
You want the people to cheer you;
in that case what is wrong
with asking them when they hear you
to say whether they like your song?
Both art and people would bloom and
grow
if that were done. Hans Sachs thinks so!

VOGELGESANG

He may be right!

KOTHNER

I think he's wrong.

NACHTIGALL

The people speak, I hold my tongue.

KOTHNER

Our art is always under a cloud
when it attempts to please the crowd.

BECKMESSER

Always he has an axe to grind.
Gutter couplets, they are his kind!

POGNER

Dear Sachs! My plan is rather new.
To make more changes will not do.
I ask now what you masters advise:
do you favor both the rule and prize?

(The masters rise in assent.)

SACHS

I'm content to take your daughter's
vote.

BECKMESSER

That cobbler always gets my goat!

KOTHNER

Would somebody care to try?
Let only bachelors apply.

BECKMESSER

And why not a widower? Think of
Hans Sachs!

SACHS

No, no, dear marker! Of younger wax
he must be made than both I and you,
if Evchen's heart he wants to woo.

BECKMESSER

Than even I? Ill-mannered crank!

KOTHNER

Is someone planning to join our rank?
Has somebody asked to enter the fray?

POGNER

Now masters, the order of the day:
I'd like to recommend
a noble man and friend
who has asked that I introduce him.
He hopes that you will choose him
and call him Mastersinger now.
My noble Stolzing, come and bow.

(Walther comes forward and bows.)

BECKMESSER (aside)

Just as I thought! So that is your plan?
(aloud) Masters, I say, too late is the
man!

THE MASTERS

That's something new. A noble here?
But is it good? Or a cause for fear?
All the same, it is not a whim
if Pogner speaks for him.

KOTHNER

If you would have us receive your guest,
then first we demand a singing test.

POGNER

Though it is true I wish him luck,
I don't suggest any of our rules should
be struck.
Ask him at your leisure.

KOTHNER

Well then, may it be your pleasure:
is the house you came from respected?

POGNER

This point can be neglected.
Since I myself declare his worth;
he is of free and noble birth.
Von Stolzing, Walther, from Frankenland,
his deed and documents I hold in hand.
The final scion of his race,
he left his dear ancestral place,
and headed Nürnberg way,
where he would like to stay.

BECKMESSER

Such noble stinkweed . . . evil stuff!

NACHTIGALL

Friend Pogner's word is quite enough.

SACHS

It's true that the masters have long
agreed:
to rank or station we pay no heed.
He who can win an artist's fame
may win the Mastersinger's name.

KOTHNER

D'rum nun frag' ich zur Stell':
welch' Meister's seid ihr Gesell'?

WALTHER

Am stillen Herd in Winterszeit,
wann Burg und Hof mir ein-
  geschneit,
wie einst der Lenz so lieblich lacht',
und wie er bald wohl neu erwacht',
ein altes Buch, vom Ahn' vermacht,
gab das mir oft zu lesen:
Herr Walther von der Vogelweid',
der ist mein Meister gewesen.

SACHS

Ein guter Meister!

BECKMESSER

Doch lang' schon tot;
wie lehrt' ihm der wohl der Regeln
  Gebot?

KOTHNER

Doch in welcher Schul' das Singen
mocht' euch zu lernen gelingen?

WALTHER

Wann dann die Flur vom Frost befreit,
und wiederkehrt die Sommerzeit,
was einst in langer Winternacht
das alte Buch mir kund gemacht,
das schallte laut in Waldespracht,
das hört' ich hell erklingen:
im Wald dort auf der Vogelweid',
da lernt' ich auch das Singen.

BECKMESSER

Oho! Von Finken und Meisen
lerntet ihr Meisterweisen?
Das wird dann wohl auch darnach sein!

VOGELGESANG

Zwei art'ge Stollen fasst' er da ein.

BECKMESSER

Ihr lobt ihn, Meister Vogelgesang?
Wohl weil vom Vogel er lernt' den Gesang?

KOTHNER

Was meint ihr, Meister? Frag' ich noch
  fort?
Mich dünkt, der Junker ist fehl am Ort.

SACHS

Das wird sich bäldlich zeigen:
wenn rechte Kunst ihm eigen
und gut er sie bewährt,
was gilt's, wer sie ihm gelehrt?

KOTHNER

Seid ihr bereit, ob euch geriet
mit neuer Find' ein Meisterlied,
nach Dicht' und Weis' eu'r eigen,
zur Stunde jetzt zu zeigen?

WALTHER

Was Winternacht,
was Waldespracht,
was Buch und Hain mich wiesen,
was Dichtersanges Wundermacht
mir heimlich wollt' erschliessen;
was Rosses Schritt
beim Waffenritt,
was Reihentanz
bei heit'rem Schanz
mir sinnend gab zu lauschen:
gilt es des Lebens höchsten Preis
um Sang mir einzutauschen,
zu eig'nem Wort, und eig'ner Weis'
will einig mir es fliessen,
als Meistersang, ob den ich weiss,
euch Meistern sich ergiessen.

BECKMESSER

Entnahmt ihr was der Worte Schwall?

VOGELGESANG

Ei nun, er wagt's!

NACHTIGALL

Merkwürd'ger Fall!

KOTHNER

Nun, Meister, wenn's gefällt,
werd' das Gemerk bestellt.
Wählt der Herr einen heil'gen Stoff?

WALTHER

Was heilig mir,
der Liebe Panier
schwing' und sing' ich, mir zu Hoff!

KOTHNER

Das gilt uns weltlich. Drum allein,
Meister Beckmesser schliesst euch ein!

BECKMESSER

(*aufstehend und widerwillig dem
  Gemerk zuschreitend*)

Ein saures Amt und heut' zumal!
Wohl gibt's mit der Kreide manche
  Qual.
Herr Ritter, wisst:
Sixtus Beckmesser Merker ist;
hier im Gemerk
verrichtet er still sein strenges Werk.
Sieben Fehler gibt er euch vor,
die merkt er mit Kreide dort an:

KOTHNER

Let me ask for a start:
which master taught you your art?

WALTHER

In wintertime, my hearth aglow,
my land and castle deep in snow,
I often read of spring's delight,
awakening after darkest night:
a book bequeathed by ancient right,
I never tired of perusing,
and Walther von der Vogelweid'
has been the master of my choosing.

SACHS

A splendid master.

BECKMESSER

But long demised.
I wonder what rules he may have ad-
vised!

KOTHNER

Tell us how you have succeeded
in learning the singing you needed.

WALTHER

When all the fields in milder clime
turned green again in summertime,
what once, in winters long and cold
that ancient book made me behold,
began to sing in sunny gold;
I heard the forest ringing.
The lovely woods on the Vogelweid'
that's where I learned my singing.

BECKMESSER

If birds and other such creatures
figure among your teachers,
I'll wager your art must be great!

VOGELGESANG

Those pretty stanzas sounded first-rate.

BECKMESSER

If you admire the song you have heard,
that's just because you were named for
a bird!

KOTHNER

What say you, masters, need I ask
more?
I fear our friend must be shown the
door.

SACHS

But first we must discover
if he's a true art lover;
if sound his tune and thought,
who cares by whom he was taught?

KOTHNER

Are you prepared to go along
and sing a brand new mastersong,
by you alone created,
with words and tune well mated?

WALTHER

What winternight,
what woods' delight,
what brook and meadow told me,
what poets' songs with their wondrous
    might
revealed to me to enfold me,
what prancing steed,
what battle's need,
what roundelay
and dancers gay
have made me hear and ponder . . .
if now my song can gain for me
this prize beyond all wonder,
I'll set my words, my melody,
to tell you what they told me.
A mastersong, if such it be,
will show you what enthralled me.

BECKMESSER

Did you find meaning in that maze?

VOGELGESANG

Oh well . . . He'll try!

NACHTIGALL

Outlandish case!

KOTHNER

Now, masters, I suggest
that we prepare the test.
Are you choosing a sacred song?

WALTHER

Of love I'll sing,
a very sacred thing.
May it win me that for which I long!

KOTHNER

We call that worldly. By the rule,
master Beckmesser, mount your stool!

BECKMESSER

(rises and goes as if unwillingly to the
    marker's booth)
A thankless task; more so today!
My slate will be suffering much dismay!
My noble peer:
Sixtus Beckmesser is marker here!
Here in his booth
he sits and records the brutal truth.
Seven errors won't spoil your score.
He'll mark them with chalk on his slate.

wenn er über sieben Fehler verlor,
dann versang der Herr Rittersmann.
Gar fein er hört;
doch dass er euch den Mut nicht stört,
säh't ihr ihm zu,
so gibt er euch Ruh',
und schliesst sich gar hier ein,
lässt Gott euch befohlen sein.

*(Er hat sich in das Gemerk gesetzt,
streckt den Kopf höhnisch freundlich
nickend heraus, und zieht den vor-
deren Vorhang zusammen, so dass er
unsichtbar wird.)*

KOTHNER *(zu Walther)*

Was euch zum Liede Richt' und
　Schnur,
vernehmt nun aus der Tabulatur.

(Er liest.)

"Ein jedes Meistergesanges Bar
stell' ordentlich ein Gemässe dar
aus unterschiedlichen Gesätzen,
die keiner soll verletzen.
Ein Gesätz besteht aus zweenen Stollen,
die gleiche Melodei haben sollen;
der Stoll' aus etlicher Vers' Gebänd,
der Vers hat einen Reim am End'.
Darauf so folgt der Abgesang,
der sei auch etlich' Verse lang,
und hab' sein' besond're Melodei,
als nicht im Stollen zu finden sei.
Derlei Gemässes mehre Baren
soll ein jed' Meisterlied bewahren;
und wer ein neues Lied gericht',
das über vier der Silben nicht
eingreift in and'rer Meister Weis',
dess' Lied erwerb' sich Meisterpreis."
Nun setzt euch in den Singestuhl!

WALTHER

Hier in den Stuhl?

KOTHNER

Wie's Brauch der Schul'.

WALTHER
(setzt sich mit Missbehagen)

Für dich, Geliebte, sei's getan!

KOTHNER

Der Sänger sitzt.

BECKMESSER *(im Gemerk)*

Fanget an!

WALTHER

"Fanget an!"
So rief der Lenz in den Wald,
dass laut es ihn durchhallt
und wie in fern'ren Wellen
der Hall von dannen flieht,
von weither nah't ein Schwellen,
das mächtig näher zieht.
Es schwillt und schallt,
es tönt der Wald
von holder Stimmen Gemenge;
nun laut und hell,
schon nah' zur Stell',
wie wächst der Schwall!
Wie Glockenhall
ertost des Jubels Gedränge!
Der Wald,
wie bald
antwortet er dem Ruf,
der neu ihm Leben schuf'
stimmte an
das süsse Lenzeslied.

*(Man hört aus dem Gemerk unmutige
Seufzer des Merkers, und heftiges
Anstreichen mit der Kreide. — Auch
Walther hat es gehört; nach kurzer
Störung fährt er fort.)*

In einer Dornenhecken,
von Neid und Gram verzehrt,
musst' er sich da verstecken,
der Winter, Grimm-bewehrt:
von dürrem Laub umrauscht,
er lauert da und lauscht,
wie er das frohe Singen
zu Schaden könnte bringen!

(Er steht vom Stuhle auf.)

Doch: fanget an!
So rief es mir in der Brust,
als noch ich von Liebe nicht wusst.
Da fühlt' ich's tief sich regen,
als weckt' es mich aus dem Traum;
mein Herz mit bebenden Schlägen
erfüllte des Busen's Raum:
das Blut, es wallt
mit Allgewalt,
geschwellt von neuem Gefühle;
aus warmer Nacht,
mit Übermacht
schwillt mir zum Meer
der Seufzer Heer
in wildem Wonnegewühle.
Die Brust
mit Lust
antwortet sie dem Ruf,
der neu ihr Leben schuf;
stimmt nun an
das hehre Liebeslied.

If you make as much as one error more,
then you know what will be your fate.

(*He sits in the booth.*)

Keen is his ear;
but, so you won't be gripped by fear
seeing him write, he moves out of sight,
and hides right in this place,
entrusting you to heaven's grace.

(*He puts out his head with a mocking
friendly nod and then disappears behind the drawn curtains of the
booth.*)

KOTHNER (*to Walther*)

So that you won't break any rule,
I now will read the laws of the school!

(*He reads.*)

"A song, to win in this master school,
must follow some old established rule,
consist of several different stanzas
and no extravaganzas.
Every stanza must contain two
        couplets;
their tune must sound as if they were
        doublets;
and each to several verses extend;
each verse must have a rhyme at its
        end.
And then you have an after-song,
also several verses long,
which must have a tune all of its own
that from the couplet is not yet known.
This kind of stanza forms the gist of
what all the mastersongs consist of;
and he who finds a song that's new,
and never borrows more than a few
conceits from other masters' lays—
his song will win the masters' praise!"
Be seated on the singer's stool.

WALTHER

Here . . . on this stool?

KOTHNER

That is the rule!

WALTHER

(*seating himself reluctantly*)

For you, beloved, I'll give in!

KOTHNER

The singer sits.

BECKMESSER (*invisible, in the booth*)

Now begin!

WALTHER

"Now begin!"
Thus cried the voices of spring;
the woods began to sing.
The singing floats and billows,
too far for any ear.
Through oaks and firs and willows,
a mighty sound draws near.
It soars and sounds,
the air abounds,
how sweet and tender the voices;
now clear and strong,
a mounting song,
it grows and swells
like ringing bells;
the forest storms and rejoices.
The song,
ere long,
rang out from all the trees,
and, praising life's new lease,
it intoned
the sweetest song of spring.

(*From the booth are heard the marker's
sighs of ill humor and vigorous
scratching of the chalk; Walther
hears it too. After a few moments of
discomposure he continues.*)

But by the forest's edges
the hoary winter sighs;
behind the thorny hedges
he hides his jealous eyes.
Around his yellowed leaves
an evil groan he heaves,
to turn this jubilation
to deepest desperation!

(*He stands up.*)

Yes, "Now begin!"
My soul replied to the call
though I never knew love at all.
My deepest thought resounded,
as though I woke from a dream,
my heart responded and pounded,
elated with joy supreme;
my seething blood,
in sweeping flood,
is swelled with unknown sensation;
through summer's night
with higher might
oceans of sighs
like waves arise,
to soar in wild exultation.
And soon
my heart takes up this lovely strain
that gave it life again,
and intones
the noble song of love!

BECKMESSER

(*den Vorhang aufreissend*)
Seid ihr nun fertig?

WALTHER

Wie fraget ihr?

BECKMESSER

Mit der Tafel ward ich fertig schier.

(*Er hält die ganz mit Kreidestrichen
bedeckte Tafel heraus; die Meister
brechen in ein Gelächter aus.*)

WALTHER

Hört doch zu meiner Frauen Preis
gelang' ich jetzt erst mit der Weis'.

BECKMESSER (*das Gemerk verlassend*)

Singt, wo ihr wollt! Hier habt ihr vertan.
Ihr Meister, schaut die Tafel euch an:
so lang' ich leb', ward's nicht erhört!
Ich glaubt's nicht, wenn ihr's all' auch
schwört!

WALTHER

Erlaubt ihr's, Meister, dass er mich
stört?
Blieb' ich von allen ungehört?

KOTHNER

Ein Wort, Herr Merker. Ihr seid
gereizt?

BECKMESSER

Sei Merker fortan, wer darnach geizt.
Doch dass der Junker versungen hat,
beleg' ich erst noch vor der Meister
Rat.
Zwar wird's 'ne harte Arbeit sein:
wo beginnen, da wo nicht aus noch ein?
Von falscher Zahl und falschem
Gebänd'
schweig' ich schon ganz und gar:
zu kurz, zu lang, wer ein End' da fänd!
Wer meint hier im Ernst einen Bar?
Auf "blinde Meinung" klag' ich allein.
Sagt, konnt' ein Sinn unsinniger sein?

MEHRERE MEISTER

Man ward nicht klug ; ich muss
gesteh'n,
ein Ende konnte keiner erseh'n.

BECKMESSER

Und dann die Weis'! Welch' tolles Ge-
kreis'
aus "Abenteuer" "blau Rittersporn"
Weis',
"hoch Tannen," "stolz Jünglings"-Ton!

KOTHNER

Ja, ich verstand gar nichts davon!

BECKMESSER

Kein Absatz wo, kein' Koloratur,
von Melodei auch nicht eine Spur!

MEHRERE MEISTER

Wer nennt das Gesang?
Es ward einem bang!
Eitel Ohrgeschinder!
Und gar nichts dahinter!

KOTHNER

Und gar vom Singstuhl ist er gesprun-
gen!

BECKMESSER

Wird erst auf die Fehlerprobe ge-
drungen?
Oder gleich erklärt, dass er versungen?

SACHS

Halt! Meister! Nicht so geeilt!
Nicht jeder eure Meinung teilt.
Des Ritters Lied und Weise,
sie fand ich neu, doch nicht verwirrt;
verliess er uns're G'leise,
schritt er doch fest und unbeirrt.
Wollt ihr nach Regeln messen,
was nicht nach eurer Regeln Lauf,
der eig'nen Spur vergessen,
sucht davon erst die Regeln auf!

BECKMESSER

Aha, schon recht! Nun hört ihr's doch:
den Stümpern öffnet Sachs ein Loch,
da aus und ein nach Belieben
ihr Wesen leicht sie trieben.
Singet dem Volk auf Markt und Gassen!
Hier wird nach den Regeln nur einge-
lassen.

SACHS

Herr Merker, was doch solch ein Eifer?
Was doch so wenig Ruh'?
Eu'r Urteil, dünkt mich, wäre reifer,
hörtet ihr besser zu.
Darum so komm' ich jetzt zum Schluss,
dass den Junker man zu End' hören
muss.

BECKMESSER

(*tearing open the curtains*)

Is this the end, now?

WALTHER

How do you dare?

BECKMESSER

On my blackboard there's no room to spare!

(*He holds out the slate quite covered with chalk marks; the Masters break out in laughter.*)

WALTHER

But hear! Once more my voice I raise
to laud the fairest with my praise.

BECKMESSER (*leaving the booth*)

Sing where you like! But here you're undone!
My masters, look how far this has gone.
Why, such a thing I've never heard!
I'd doubt it, though you gave your word!

WALTHER

I ask you, masters, can he be curbed,
that you might hear me undisturbed?

POGNER

One word, good marker . . . why are you vexed?

BECKMESSER

I don't care who may be marker next,
but that our noble friend has lost his case
I'll prove to all the masters phrase by phrase.
Though that will be a heavy chore—
there's no telling what's after, what's before!
Of faulty beats bar after bar
let us not even speak . . .
too short, too long: who can count that far?
It might just as well have been Greek.
I plead "no meaning", just hit or miss.
Where is there sense in nonsense like this?

SEVERAL MASTERS

It made no sense, I must admit!
There was no word nor sound that would fit.

BECKMESSER

And then the sound,
the craziest round
of daring venture,
blue horseman's spur tune,
of pine tree, proud youngster call!

KOTHNER

I understood nothing at all.

BECKMESSER

No single rest, no coloratura line,
of melody and tune not even a sign!

SOME MASTERS

A treat for the ear!
It filled me with fear!
Every ear was shattered!
And nothing that mattered!

KOTHNER

He left his chair, too, that should be listed!

BECKMESSER

I'd cite all his errors if you insisted!
He has had his chance, and he has missed it!

SACHS

Please, masters! Why all this haste?
Not everybody shares your taste.
The singer's bold intention
I found quite new, but hardly wrong.
Though he has scorned convention,
his pace was firm, assured, and strong.
If you want rules to measure
what lies beyond your rules' decree,
for what is new and fresher
first find out what the rules might be!

BECKMESSER

Aha, I see! It's very clear.
Hans Sachs invites the bunglers here.
Indeed, it would be enchanting
to hear those bunglers ranting!
Sing in the streets if you want to please the masses!
Here only the rules can tell us who passes.

SACHS

Friend marker, tell me, why this fluster?
You are upset, I fear,
your judgment would be so much juster
if you would lend an ear.
And this will be my final word:
the remainder of his song must be heard.

BECKMESSER

Die Meister Zunft, die ganze Schul'
gegen den Sachs da sind wir Null.

SACHS

Verhüt es Gott, was ich begehr',
dass das nicht nach den Gesetzen wär'!
Doch da nun steht geschrieben:
"Der Merker werde so bestellt,
dass weder Hass noch Lieben
das Urteil trübe, das er fällt."
Geht der nun gar auf Freiersfüssen
wie sollt' er da die Lust nicht büssen,
den Nebenbuhler auf dem Stuhl
zu schmähen vor der ganzen Schul'?

NACHTIGALL

Ihr geht zu weit!

KOTHNER

Persönlichkeit!

POGNER

Vermeidet, Meister, Zwist und Streit!

BECKMESSER

Ei, was kümmert's doch Meister Sachsen,
auf was für Füssen ich geh'?
Liess' er doch lieber Sorge sich wachsen,
dass mir nichts drück' die Zeh'!
Doch seit mein Schuster ein grosser
Poet,
gar übel es um mein Schuhwerk steht:
da seht, wie's schlappt,
und überall klappt!
All' seine Vers' und Reim'
liess ich ihm gern daheim,
Historien, Spiel' und Schwänke dazu,
bracht' er mir morgen die neuen
Schuh'!

SACHS

Ihr mahnt mich da gar recht,
doch schickt sich's, Meister, sprecht,
dass, find ich selbst dem Eseltreiber
ein Sprüchlein auf die Sohl',
dem hochgelahrten Herrn Stadtschreiber
ich nichts d'rauf schreiben soll?
Das Sprüchlein, das eu'r würdig sei,
mit all' meiner armen Poeterei
fand ich noch nicht zur Stund';
doch wird's wohl jetzt mir kund,
wenn ich des Ritters Lied gehört:
d'rum sing' er nur weiter ungestört!

(WALTHER, *in grosser Aufregung, steigt
auf den Singstuhl.*)

DIE MEISTER

Nicht weiter! Genug! Zum Schluss!

SACHS (*zu Walther*)

Singt dem Herrn Merker zum Verdruss!

BECKMESSER

Was sollte man da noch hören?
Wär's nicht euch zu betören?
Jeden Fehler gross und klein,
seht genau auf der Tafel ein.
"Falsch Gebänd," "unredbare Worte,"
"Kleb-Silben," hier "Laster" gar;
"Aequivoca," "Reim am falschen Orte,"
"Verkehrt," "verstellt" der ganze Bar.
Ein "Flickgesang" hier zwischen den
Stollen!
"Blinde Meinung" allüberall!
"Unklare Wort'," "Differenz," hie
"Schrollen!"
Da "falscher Atem," hier "Überfall."
Ganz unverständliche Melodei.
Aus allen Tönen ein Mischgebräu'!
Scheu'tet ihr nicht das Ungemach,
Meister, zählt mir die Striche nach!
Verloren hätt' er schon mit dem Acht',
doch so weit wie der hat's noch keiner
gebracht:
wohl über fünfzig, schlecht gezählt!
Sagt, ob ihr euch den zum Meister
wählt?

DIE MEISTER (*durcheinander*)

Jawohl, so ist's! Ich seh' es recht!
Mit dem Herrn Ritter steht es schlecht.
Mag Sachs von ihm halten, was er will,
hier in der Singschul' schweig' er still!
Bleibt einem Jeden doch unbenommen,
wen er sich zum Genossen begehrt?
Wär' uns der erste best' willkommen,
was blieben die Meister noch wert?
Hei! Wie sich der Ritter da quält!
Der Sachs hat sich ihn erwählt.
'S ist ärgerlich gar! D'rum macht ein
End'!
Auf, Meister! Simmt, und erhebt die
Händ'!

POGNER

Jawohl, ich seh's, was mir nicht recht:
mit meinem Junker steht es schlecht!
Weich' ich hier der Übermacht,
mir ahnet, dass mir's Sorge macht.
Wie gern säh' ich ihn angenommen,
als Eidam wär' er mir gar wert;
nenn' ich den Sieger jetzt willkommen,
wer weiss, ob ihn mein Kind begehrt!
Gesteh' ich's, dass mich's quält
ob Eva den Meister wählt!

BECKMESSER

The masters' guild, we singers proud,
one word from Sachs and we are
  cowed!

SACHS

May God forbid that I should look
for any favors against the book!
That book says in one section:
"The marker shall be chosen such
that hatred or affection
must never guide him as a judge."
Now, if your marker plans to marry,
I ask you, friends, why would he tarry
to bait his rival on the stool
and tear him down before the school?

NACHTIGALL

You go too far!

KOTHNER

Now, please, no names!

POGNER

I beg you, master, let us not spar!

BECKMESSER

Why, I ask you, should Sachs be sorry
that I might wed if I chose?
I suggest he should much rather worry
that nothing pinches my toes!
But since my shoemaker also makes
  verse,
for all his verses my shoes are worse,
You see, they snap,
they wiggle and flap.
All he is rhyming about
I could do gladly without;
the ballads, pranks, and whims of his
  muse,
if by tomorrow I'd get my shoes!

SACHS

You're right, I must admit,
but do you think it fit
that, though I write the donkeydriver
a ditty on his shoes,
our learned marker and townwriter
should be without my muse?
The verse that might be worthy of you,
despite all the humble rhyming I do,
so far I did not find.
But now it comes to mind
as by this lovely song I'm swayed,
so let him continue undismayed!

(*Walther mounts the singer's chair in
  great excitement.*)

THE MASTERS

Enough! That's all!

SACHS (*to Walther*)

Sing! Never mind the marker's gall!

BECKMESSER

Let's tell him the guild refuses.
Don't listen to his ruses!
Every single time he missed!
Have a look! I have made a list!
"Wrongly built" . . . "unspeakable
  phrases"
"queer syllables!" A "faulty noun"!
"Aequivoca"! "Rhymes in awkward
  places"!
And here this verse was upside down!
A "patched-up tune" right here in the
  middle!
"Void of meaning", poorer than poor!
"Confounded words" "out of joint" a
  "riddle"
here "faulty breathing" "non sequitur"!
Incomprehensible every stress!
He made of singing a holy mess!
If you can stand the misery,
masters: count his mistakes with me!
Just eight mistakes will spoil
  any score!
He went far beyond! No one ever made
  more.
Well over fifty! That's a guess!
Who deserves the name of master less?

THE MASTERS

There is no doubt. It's pretty clear
that he can't be a master here!
Let Sachs think that he's the singers'
  king;
here in the school he cannot sing!
True, ev'ryone must be free in choosing
his own companion, quite undeterred.
But if we're cramped in our refusing
what then is a master's desert?
See how Walther Stolzing keeps on!
But Sachs believes he has won!
It's lasted too long! Time that it ends!
Come, masters, vote! By a show of
  hands.

POGNER

There is no doubt, it's very clear;
my friend has not been welcome here!
If they make me lose this fray,
I fear that I shall rue the day.
His failure would be most distressing!
He'd be a welcome son to me.
Whoever wins must have my blessing!
Who knows if Eva will agree.

WALTHER

Aus finst'rer Dornenhecken
die Eule rauscht hervor,
tät rings mit Kreischen wecken
der Raben heis'ren Chor:
in nächt'gem Heer zu Hauf
wie krächzen all' da auf,
mit ihren Stimmen, den hohlen,
die Elstern, Krähen und Dohlen!
Auf da steigt,
mit gold'nem Flügelpaar,
ein Vogel wunderbar;
sein strahlend hell Gefieder
licht in den Lüften blinkt;
schwebt selig hin und wieder,
zu Flug und Flucht mir winkt.
Es schwillt das Herz
vor süssem Schmerz
der Not entwachsen Flügel;
es schwingt sich auf
zum kühnen Lauf,
aus der Städte Gruft,
zum Flug durch die Luft
dahin zum heim'schen Hügel,
dahin zur grünen Vogelweid',
wo Meister Walther einst mich freit';
da sing' ich hell und hehr
der liebsten Frauen Ehr':
auf dann steigt,
ob Meister-Kräh'n ihm ungeneigt,
das stolze Liebeslied.
Ade! ihr Meister, hienied'!

SACHS

Ha, welch ein Mut!
Begeistrungsglut!
Ihr Meister schweigt doch und hört!
Hört, wenn Sachs euch beschwört!
Herr Merker dort, gönnt doch nur
   Ruh'!
Lasst and're hören, gebt das nur zu!
Umsonst! All eitel Trachten!
Kaum vernimmt man sein eignes Wort!
Des Junkers will keiner achten:
das nenn' ich Mut, singt der noch fort!
Das Herz auf dem rechten Fleck:
ein wahrer Dichter Reck!
Mach' ich, Hans Sachs, wohl Vers und
   Schuh',
ist Ritter der und Poet dazu.

DIE LEHRBUBEN

Glück auf zum Meistersingen,
mögt ihr euch das Kränzlein erschwingen;
das Blumenkränzlein aus Seiden fein,
wird das dem Herrn Ritter beschieden
   sein?

BECKMESSER

Nun, Meister, kündet's an!

ALLE MEISTER

Versungen und vertan!

(*Walther verlässt mit einer stolz ver-
ächtlichen Gebärde den Stuhl und
wendet sich rasch zum Fortgehen.—
Alles geht in grosser Aufregung auseinander; lustiger Tumult der Lehrbuben, welche sich des Gemerkes, des
Singstuhl's und der Meisterbänke be-
mächtigen, wodurch Gedränge und
Durcheinander der nach dem Ausgange sich wendenden Meister ent-
steht. Sachs, der allein im Vorder-
grunde geblieben, blickt noch gedan-
kenvoll nach dem leeren Singstuhl; als
die Lehrbuben auch diesen erfassen,
und Sachs mit humoristisch un-
mutiger Gebärde sich abwendet, fällt
der Vorhang.*)

ZWEITER AUFZUG

*Die Bühne stellt im Vordergrund eine
Strasse im Längendurchschnitt dar,
welche in der Mitte von einer schma-
len Gasse, nach dem Hintergrunde zu
krumm abbiegend, durchschnitten
wird, so dass sich in Front zwei Eck-
häuser darbieten, von denen das eine,
reichere, rechts das Haus Pogner's,
das andere, einfachere, links das des
Sachs ist. Vor Pogner's Haus eine
Linde, vor dem Sachsen's ein Flieder-
baum.—Heiterer Sommerabend; im
Verlaufe der ersten Auftritte allmählich einbrechende Nacht. David ist
darüber her, die Fensterläden nach
der Gasse zu von aussen zu schliessen.
Alle Lehrbuben tun das Gleiche bei
andern Häusern.*

LEHRBUBEN (*während der Arbeit*)

Johannistag! Johannistag!
Blumen und Bänder so viel man mag!

DAVID (*für sich*)

"Das Blumenkränzlein aus Seiden fein,
möcht' es mir balde beschieden sein!"

MAGDALENE

(*ist mit einem Korbe am Arm aus Pogner's Haus gekommen*)
Bst! David!

DAVID

Ruft ihr schon wieder?
Singt allein eure dummen Lieder!

WALTHER

From dark and thorny hedges
the owl unfolds his wings;
and taking up his screeches,
a choir of ravens sings;
that mighty, nightly swarm,
its croaking turns to storm,
as every voice within reach howls,
the magpies, jackdaws and screech-
    owls!
Wings of gold
that bear to dazzling height
a bird of wondrous sight,
its radiant plumage glitters,
a sheer delight to see;
and as it floats and flitters,
it bids me fly and flee.
My heart is slain with sweetest pain,
grows wings from all its pining,
it mounts and soars
in daring course
from the city's lair
it flies through the air
where homeward hills are shining;
away and home to the fowler's lea,
where master Walther set me free;
and there my voice I raise
in fairest woman's praise;
rising high,
though master crows may croak and
    cry!
The proudest hymn of love!
Farewell, you masters! Enough!

SACHS

He is inspired!
with ardor fired.
Now, masters, let him be heard!
Lend an ear to my word!
Be silent, now. You've done your task!
Let others hear him—that's all I ask!
In vain all his invention!
It's too noisy to hear one's own word!
There's no one to pay attention;
I call him brave; he's undeterred!
His heart true as true can be,
a poet hero, he!
If I, Hans Sachs, make verse and shoe,
he's nobly born and a poet too!

PRENTICES

Now here's to a glad beginning!
Here's hoping that you will be winning
the flower chaplet with silken trim,
we wonder if that will be given to him?

BECKMESSER

Now, masters! Cast your vote!

ALL MASTERS

He fumbled and he failed!

(*Walther, with a proudly contemptu-
ous gesture, leaves the chair and
quickly turns to go. General excitement, merry tumult of the Prentices
who arm themselves with pieces of
the booth, the chair and the benches,
causing confusion among the masters
who are making for the door. Sachs,
who has remained alone in the foreground, still gazes thoughtfully at the
empty singer's chair. As the boys start
to remove it, and Sachs turns away
with a humorously indignant gesture,
the curtain falls.*)

ACT TWO

*The front of the stage represents a
street in longitudinal section, inter-
sected in the middle by a narrow,
crooked alley winding towards the
back; of the two corner houses thus
presented in front, the grander one
on the right is Pogner's, the other,
simpler one, is Sachs'. Before Pogner's house is a linden tree, before
Sachs' a lilac. A genial summer evening; in the course of the first scene
night gradually falls. David is en-
gaged in closing from without the
shutters of the windows toward the
alley. All the Prentices do the same
for other houses.*

PRENTICES (*during their work*)

Midsummer Day! Midsummer Day!
Flowers and ribbons, take all you may.

DAVID (*aside*)

"The flower chaplet with silken trim,
could it be mine soon by destiny's
    whim?"

MAGDALENE

(*has come from Pogner's house with a
basket on her arm*)

Psst! David!

DAVID (*turning toward the alley*)

You think you're witty?
I don't care for your silly ditty!

LEHRBUBEN

David, was soll's?
Wär'st nicht so stolz,
schaut'st besser um,
wär'st nicht so dumm!
"Johannistag! Johannistag!"
Wie der nur die Jungfer Lene nicht
  kennen mag!

MAGDALENE

David! Hör' doch! Kehr' dich zu mir!

DAVID

Ach, Jungfer Lene! Ihr seid hier?

MAGDALENE (auf ihren Korb deutend)

Bring' dir was gut's, schau' nur hinein:
das soll für mein lieb' Schätzel sein.
Erst aber schnell, wie ging's mit dem
  Ritter?
Du rietest ihm gut? Er gewann den
  Kranz?

DAVID

Ah, Jungfer Lene! Da steht's bitter:
der hat vertan und versungen ganz!

MAGDALENE

Versungen? Vertan?

DAVID

Was geht's euch nur an?

MAGDALENE

Hand von der Taschen!
Nichts zu naschen!
Hilf Gott! Unser Junker vertan!
(Sie geht nach dem Hause zurück.)

DIE LEHRBUBEN

Heil! Heil zur Eh' dem jungen Mann!
Wie glücklich hat er gefreit!
Wir hörten's all', und sahen's an;
der er sein Herz geweiht,
für die er lässt sein Leben,
die hat ihm den Korb nicht gegeben.

DAVID (auffahrend)

Was steht ihr hier faul?
Gleich haltet das Maul!

DIE LEHRBUBEN (David umtanzend)

Johannistag! Johannistag!
Da freit ein Jeder, wie er mag.
Der Meister freit!
Der Bursche freit!
Da gibt's Geschlamb' und Geschlumb-
  fer!

Der Alte freit
die junge Maid,
der Bursche die alte Jumbfer!
Juchhei! Juchhei! Johannistag!

SACHS (kommt aus der Gasse)

Was gibt's? Treff' ich dich wieder am
  Schlag?

DAVID

Nicht ich! Schandlieder singen die.

SACHS

Hör' nicht d'rauf! Lern's besser wie sie!
Zur Ruh', in's Haus! Schliess' und
  mach' Licht!

DAVID

Hab' ich noch Singstund'?

SACHS

Nein, singst nicht
zur Straf' für dein heutig' frech
  Erdreisten.
Die neuen Schuh' steck' mir auf den
  Leisten!
(Sie sind beide in die Werkstatt einge-
treten. Pogner und Eva, vom Spazier-
gange heimkehrend, sind die Gasse
heraufgekommen.)

POGNER

Lass seh'n, ob Nachbar Sachs zu Haus?
Gern spräch' ich ihn. Trät' ich wohl
  ein?
(David kommt mit Licht aus der Kam-
mer, setzt sich an den Werktisch am
Fenster and macht sich über die
Arbeit her.)

EVA

Er scheint daheim: kommt Licht
  heraus.

POGNER

Tu' ich's? Zu was doch? Besser nein.
Will einer Selt'nes wagen,
was liess' er sich dann sagen?
War er's nicht, der meint', ich ging' zu
  weit?
Und blieb ich nicht im Geleise,
war's nicht auf seine Weise?
Doch war's vielleicht auch Eitelkeit?
Und du, mein Kind? Du sagst mir
  nichts?

EVA

Ein folgsam Kind, gefragt nur spricht's.

POGNER

Wie klug! Wie gut! Komm', setz' dich
  hier
ein' Weil' noch auf die Bank zu mir.

EVA

Wird's nicht zu kühl?
'S war heut' gar schwül.

PRENTICES

David, what's that?
Blind as a bat!
You might be wise
to use your eyes!
"Midsummer Day! Midsummer Day!"
How dumb not to see his Lene across
 the way!

MAGDALENE

David! Listen! Do turn around!

DAVID

Ah, Magdalene, you are here!

MAGDALENE

(pointing to her basket)

What I have brought you will enjoy;
some goodies for my favorite boy!
How did it go? Was he in his glory?
You gave him advice? Did he win the
 crown?

DAVID

Ah! Magdalene! A sad story!
Stolzing has failed and is quite undone!

MAGDALENE

It can't be! He failed!

DAVID

How you carry on!

MAGDALENE

(pulling back the basket)

No, I won't let you!
I'll forget you!
Good Lord; Walter Stolzing has failed!
(She goes back to the house.)

PRENTICES

Hail! Hail! To a man about to wed!
None is as happy as he!
There! See the nose by which he's led:
she who was bride-to-be,
the one whom he is wooing,
she says in reply: nothing doing!

DAVID (angrily)

Now that is enough!
Why can't you be still?

PRENTICES

(dancing round David)

Midsummer Day! Midsummer Day!
When all are wooing as best they may.
The master woos,
the prentice woos,
everywhere hearts go asurgin'.

The old one woos
the youngest maid,
the young one the oldest virgin!
Hooray! Hooray! Midsummer Day!

SACHS (has come up the alley)

What's this? When will you learn to
 behave?

DAVID

Not I! They're making fun of me!

SACHS

Never mind! Be smarter than they.
Be still, lock up. Quick, bring a light!

DAVID

And then my lesson?

SACHS

Not tonight,
because your behavior was so wretched!
That pair of shoes needs a bit of
 stretching!
(David and Sachs enter the workshop
 and go off. Pogner and Eva, returning from a walk, have come up the
 alley.)

POGNER

Let's see if master Sachs is home.
A word with him would do me good.
(David comes from the inner room with
 a light, sits at the work-bench by the
 window and works.)

EVA

I see a light: he must be home.

POGNER

Shall I? I wonder. Better not.
If one is bold and daring,
he will not be forbearing.
'Twas Sachs, though, who thought I
 was too free.
But if I broke with convention,
I followed his intention.
Perhaps he spoke from vanity.
And you, my child? Have you no word?

EVA

A child, unasked, should not be heard.

POGNER

How wise! How good! Come, come
 right here,
sit down here by my side, my dear.

EVA

It might get cool . . .
The day was close.

POGNER

Nicht doch, 's ist mild und labend,
gar lieblich lind der Abend:
das deutet auf den schönsten Tag,
der morgen soll erscheinen.
O Kind, sagt dir kein Herzensschlag,
welch' Glück dich morgen treffen mag,
wenn Nürenberg, die ganze Stadt,
mit Bürgern und Gemeinen,
mit Zünften, Volk und hohem Rat
vor dir sich soll vereinen,
dass du den Preis,
das edle Reis,
erteilest als Gemahl
dem Meister deiner Wahl?

EVA

Lieb' Vater, muss es ein Meister sein?

POGNER

Hör' wohl: ein Meister deiner Wahl.
(*Magdalene erscheint an der Tür und
winkt Eva.*)

EVA (*zerstreut*)

Ja, meiner Wahl. Doch tritt nun ein
(gleich, Lene, gleich!) zum Abendmahl.

POGNER *ärgerlich*)

's gibt doch keinen Gast?

EVA

Wohl den Junker?

POGNER (*halb für sich*)

Wie so?

EVA

Sahst ihn heut' nicht?

POGNER (*halb für sich*)

Ward sein' nicht froh.
Nicht doch! Was denn? Ei! Werd' ich
dumm?

EVA

Lieb Väterchen, komm! Geh', kleid'
dich um.

POGNER (*in das Haus gehend*)

Hm! Was geht mir im Kopf doch 'rum?

MAGDALENE (*heimlich*)

Hast was heraus?

EVA

Blieb still und stumm.

MAGDALENE

Sprach David: meint', er habe vertan.

EVA

Der Ritter? Hilf Gott, was fing' ich an?
Ach, Lene; die Angst! Wo was erfah-
ren?

MAGDALENE

Vielleicht vom Sachs?

EVA

Ach, der hat mich lieb!
Gewiss, ich geh' hin.

MAGDALENE

Lass' drin nichts gewahren;
der Vater merkt' es, wenn man jetzt
blieb'.
Nach dem Mahl: dann hab' ich dir
noch 'was zu sagen,
was jemand geheim mir aufgetragen.

EVA

Wer denn? Der Junker?

MAGDALENE

Nichts da! Nein! Beckmesser.

EVA

Das mag 'was Rechtes sein!
(*Sie gehen in das Haus.*)
(*Sachs ist in die Werkstatt zurück-
gekommen.*)

SACHS

Zeig' her, 's ist gut. Dort an die Tür'
rück' mir Tisch und Schemel herfür.
Leg' dich zu Bett, steh' auf bei Zeit;
verschlaf' die Dummheit, sei morgen
gescheit!

DAVID (*richtet Tisch und Schemel*)

Schafft ihr noch Arbeit?

SACHS

Kümmert dich das?

DAVID (*für sich*)

Was war nur der Lene? Gott weiss,
was!
Warum wohl der Meister heute wacht?

SACHS

Was steh'st noch?

DAVID

Schlaft wohl, Meister!

SACHS

Gut' Nacht!
(*David geht in die Kammer ab.*)

POGNER

Oh no, it's mild and balmy,
a night to soothe and calm me.
A token of the fairest day,
tomorrow's expectation.
My child! Does not your heartbeat say
what happiness may come your way
when Nürnberg, the city proud,
its folks of every station,
the guilds, the council, and the crowd
will grant their acclamation,
when you bestow the noble bough,
proclaim with steady voice
the master of your choice?

EVA

Dear father, must I be a master's bride?

POGNER

I said: a master of your choice.
(*Magdalene appears at the door and
beckons to Eva.*)

EVA (*distractedly*)

Yes, of my choice. Let's go inside,
(yes, Lene, yes) it's dinner time.

POGNER (*irritated*)

We don't have a guest?

EVA

Walther Stolzing?

POGNER (*surprised*)

What's that?

EVA

Was he not there?

POGNER (*half aside*)

He was, alas.
But no . . . what's this? Why . . . what
a thought!

EVA

Come, father dear, come. Go change
your coat.

POGNER

Why . . . what's going around in my
head? (*goes into his house*)

MAGDALENE (*secretly to Eva*)

Did you find out?

EVA

No word was said.

MAGDALENE

My David says he thinks he has failed.

EVA

He said that? Good Lord! What shall
I do?
I am so afraid! Where shall I turn
now?

MAGDALENE

Perhaps to Sachs!

EVA

Yes, he's such a dear!
That's it! I will go.

MAGDALENE

But think of your father,
he gets suspicious if we stay here . . .
better wait: you also must pay some
attention
to a secret that I was asked to mention.

EVA

By whom? By Stolzing?

MAGDALENE

Stolzing? No! Beckmesser!

EVA

Well, I can hardly wait!
(*They go into the house.*)

SACHS

(*has returned to the shop*)

Let's see . . . That's fine. Now come
out here.
Put my stool, my table right here.
Now go to bed, at seven rise;
sleep off your folly, tomorrow be wise.

DAVID

(*arranging bench and stool*)

You'll go on working?

SACHS

Mind your own business.

DAVID (*aside*)

What happened to Lene? Heaven
knows!
But why should the master stay awake?

SACHS

That is all.

DAVID

Sleep well, Master!

SACHS

Good night!
(*David goes into his room.*)

SACHS
*(legt sich die Arbeit zurecht, setzt sich
an der Türe auf den Schemel, lässt
dann die Arbeit wieder liegen, und
lehnt sich zurück)*
Wie duftet doch der Flieder
so mild, so stark und voll!
Mir löst er weich die Glieder,
will, dass ich was sagen soll.
Was gilt's, was ich dir sagen kann?
Bin gar ein arm einfältig' Mann!
Soll mir die Arbeit nicht schmecken,
gäb'st, Freund, lieber mich frei:
tät' besser, das Leder zu strecken,
und liess alle Poëterei!
Und doch, 's will halt nicht geh'n.
Ich fühl's und kann's nicht versteh'n,
kann's nicht behalten, doch auch nicht
    vergessen:
und fass' ich es ganz, kann ich's nicht
    messen!
Doch wie wollt' ich auch fassen,
was unermesslich mir schien.
Kein' Regel wollte da passen,
und war doch kein Fehler d'rin.
Es klang so alt und war doch so neu,
wie Vogelsang im süssen Mai!
Wer ihn hört,
und wahnbetört
sänge dem Vogel nach,
dem brächt' es Spott und Schmach.
Lenzes Gebot,
die süsse Not,
die legt es ihm in die Brust:
nun sang er, wie er musst;
und wie er musst', so konnt' er's;
das merkt' ich ganz besonders.
Dem Vogel, der heut' sang,
dem war der Schnabel hold gewachsen,
macht' er den Meistern bang,
gar wohl gefiel er doch Hans Sachsen.
*(Eva ist auf die Strasse getreten und
steht jetzt unvermerkt an der Türe
bei Sachs.)*
EVA
Gut'n Abend, Meister; noch so fleissig?
SACHS
(ist angenehm überrascht aufgefahren)
Ei, Kind! Lieb' Evchen! Noch so spät?
Und doch, warum so spät noch, weiss
ich: die neuen Schuh'?
EVA
Wie fehl er rät!
Die Schuh' hab' ich noch gar nicht pro-
    biert;
sie sind so schön und reich geziert,
dass ich sie noch nicht an die Füss'
    mir getraut.

SACHS
Doch sollst sie morgen tragen als Braut?
EVA
Wer wäre denn Bräutigam?
SACHS
Weiss ich das?
EVA
Wie wisst ihr dann, dass ich Braut?
SACHS
Ei was! Das weiss die Stadt.
EVA
Ja, weiss es die Stadt,
Freund Sachs gute Gewähr dann hat.
Ich dacht', er wüsst' mehr.
SACHS
Was soll ich wissen?
EVA
Ei, seht doch! Werd' ich's ihm sagen
    müssen?
Ich bin wohl recht dumm?
SACHS
Das sagt' ich nicht.
EVA
Dann wär't ihr wohl klug?
SACHS
Das weiss ich nicht.
EVA
Ihr wisst nichts? Ihr sagt nichts? Ei,
    Freund Sachs
jetzt merk' ich wahrlich, Pech is kein
    Wachs.
Ich hätt' euch für feiner gehalten.
SACHS
Kind, beid', Wachs und Pech bekannt
    mir sind:
mit Wachs strich ich die seid'nen
    Fäden,
damit ich dir die zieren Schuh' gefasst:
heut' fass ich die Schuh' mit dicht'ren
    Drähten,
da gilt's mit Pech für den derb'ren
    Gast.
EVA
Wer ist denn der? Wohl 'was recht's?
SACHS
Das mein' ich!
Ein Meister stolz auf Freier's Fuss,
denkt morgen zu siegen ganz alleinig:
Herrn Beckmesser's Schuh' ich richten
muss.

SACHS

(arranges his work, sits on the stool at the door, then lays down his work again and leans back)

The lilac's scent, how tender,
how mild, how full today!
It bids my heart surrender,
grope for a few words to say.
And yet, such words are hard to find
for one like me, simple of mind.
Give up my work altogether?
No, friend, that would not do.
Much better to stretch my leather,
forget all the poems I knew!
And yet, it will not go.
I feel, but never shall know;
I can't retain it, nor can I forget it.
And even if grasped, it has no measure.
How could I ever measure
what all measure seems to defy.
The masters' rules would not fit it,
and yet there was no mistake.
A sound so old and yet it was new,
like birds that sing when spring breaks
    through!
He who heard that wondrous bird,
were he to sing the same,
would reap but scorn and shame.
Spring did ordain;
the sweetest pain
inspired him deep in his heart.
It taught him how to start.
And he could sing as he had to.
Hans Sachs has noticed that, too.
The bird who sang today . . .
his beak was grown to noble measure.
Masters voiced their dismay,
and yet Hans Sachs admits his pleasure!

(Eva has come into the street and stands unnoticed by Sachs' door.)

EVA

Good evening, master! Time you
rested?

SACHS

(starts in agreeable surprise)

My child, dear Evchen, still awake?
But wait, I think I may have guessed it:
it is your shoes?

EVA

How you mistake!
In fact, I've never put them yet on.
They are so fine, so richly done,
such beautiful shoes are too good to be
tried.

SACHS

But you are soon to wear them as a
bride.

EVA

And who might the husband be?

SACHS

I don't know.

EVA

Then how d'you know I'll be bride?

SACHS

My child, everyone knows.

EVA

Why, if that is so,
that explains how Hans Sachs would
    know.
I thought he'd know more.

SACHS

What's that I would know?

EVA

You ask me what it might be you should
    know.
I must be a fool.

SACHS

I don't say that.

EVA

Then you must be wise.

SACHS

I don't know that.

EVA

You don't know? You don't say? Yes,
friend Sachs,
I understand now: pitch is not wax.
I truly had thought you were keener.

SACHS

Child, both wax and pitch I too can
tell.
With wax, sewing your shoes, untiring,
with wax I tried to smoothe their every
    stitch;
but now I make shoes with stronger
    wiring;
the cruder customer needs some pitch.

EVA

And who is that? Someone great?

SACHS

The greatest!
A master proud enough to woo.
He's sure he can win you as a poet,
it's Beckmesser's foot will wear this shoe.

EVA

So nehmt nur tüchtig Pech dazu:
da kleb' er drin und lass' mir Ruh'!

SACHS

Er hofft dich sicher zu ersingen.

EVA

Wie so denn der?

SACHS

Ein Junggesell:
's gibt deren wenig dort zur Stell'.

EVA

Könnt's einem Witwer nicht gelingen?

SACHS

Mein Kind, der wär' zu alt für dich.

EVA

Ei was! Zu alt? Hier gilt's der Kunst
wer sie versteht, der werb' um mich.

SACHS

Lieb' Evchen machst mir blauen
Dunst?

EVA

Nicht ich, ihr seid's, ihr macht mir
Flausen!
Gesteht nur, dass ihr wandelbar;
Gott weiss, wer euch jetzt im Herzen
mag hausen!
Glaubt' ich mich doch drin so manches
Jahr.

SACHS

Wohl, da ich dich gern auf den
Armen trug?

EVA

Ich seh', 's war nur, weil ihr kinderlos.

SACHS

Hatt' einst ein Weib und Kinder
genug.

EVA

Doch starb eure Frau, so wuchs ich
gross?

SACHS

Gar gross und schön.

EVA

Da dacht' ich aus,
ihr nähm't mich für Weib und Kind
in's Haus?

SACHS

Da hätt ich ein Kind und auch ein
Weib!
'S wär' gar ein lieber Zeitvertreib!
Ja, ja! das hast du dir schön erdacht.

EVA

Ich glaub', der Meister mich gar ver-
lacht?
Am End' auch liess' er sich gar gefallen,
dass unter der Nas' ihm weg vor allen
der Beckmesser morgen mich ersäng?

SACHS

Wer sollt's ihm wehren, wenn's ihm ge-
läng'?
Dem wüsst' allein dein Vater Rat.

EVA

Wo so ein Meister den Kopf nur hat!
Käm' ich zu euch wohl, fänd' ich's zu
Haus?

SACHS

Ach, ja! hast Recht: 's ist im Kopf mir
kraus.
Hab' heut' manch' Sorg' und Wirr'
erlebt:
da mag's dann sein, dass was drin
klebt.

EVA

Wohl in der Singschul'? 's war heut'
Gebot.

SACHS

Ja, Kind! Eine Freiung machte mir
Not.

EVA

Ja, Sachs! das hättet ihr gleich soll'n
sagen,
quält euch dann nicht mit unnützen
Fragen.
Nun sagt, wer war's, der Freiung
begehrt?

SACHS

Ein Junker, Kind, gar unbelehrt.

EVA

Ein Junker? Mein, sagt! und ward er
gefreit?

SACHS

Nichts da, mein Kind! 'S gab gar viel
Streit.

EVA

So sagt, erzählt, wie ging es zu?
Macht's euch Sorg', wie liess' mir es
Ruh'?
So bestand er übel und hat vertan?

SACHS

Ohne Gnad' versang der Herr Rittersmann.

MAGDALENE

(*kommt zum Haus heraus und ruft
leise*)

Bst! Evchen! Bst!

EVA

Take lots of pitch so he'll be stuck,
and let me hope for better luck.

SACHS

He hopes to win you with his singing.

EVA

But why on earth?

SACHS

He's single yet,
and bachelors are hard to get.

EVA

Could not a widower be the winner?

SACHS

My child, he'd be too old for you.

EVA

But why? Too old? Where art's the test,
those who know art may come and woo.

SACHS

Dear Evchen, that's a pretty jest.

EVA

Not I, you, Sachs, you do the jesting.
Admit it: you've a fickle heart.
God alone may know who's now in
there resting.
For years I thought I had played that
part.

SACHS

Because I have borne you in my arms
before?

EVA

I was a child to a childless man.

SACHS

I had a wife and children galore.

EVA

Your wife passed away and I grew up.

SACHS

So tall and fair!

EVA

I've often dreamt:
I might be wife and child to you.

SACHS

Then I'd have a child, also a wife.
A lovely way to spend my life.
Indeed, your plans are well laid, I see.

EVA

Hans Sachs, I think you make fun of
me.
I'm certain you would not feel much
sorrow
if under your very nose tomorrow
Herr Beckmesser really won the prize.

SACHS

Who's to prevent him, if he's that wise,
unless your father changed his mind?

EVA

How can a master be deaf and blind?
If he had changed it, would I have
come?

SACHS

Ah yes, you're right, in my head all's
numb.
I have been quite upset today.
My head still whirls as well it may.

EVA

Was there a contest? Someone applied?

SACHS

Yes, child: by a trial I was sorely tried.

EVA

Why Sachs, if I had known what was
the matter,
I should have gladly spared you the
chatter.
Who was it? Who was the singer, I
mean?

SACHS

A nobleman, but very green.

EVA

A nobleman? Dear me! He carried the
day?

SACHS

Not so, my child. There was a fray.

EVA

Oh, please, do tell: how did he fare?
If you are worried, I, too, must care.
Did he sing so poorly? Was he so bad?

SACHS

There's no hope . . . He lost every
chance he had.

MAGDALENE

(*comes out of the house and calls
softly*)
Psst! Evchen! Psst!

EVA

Ohne Gnade? Wie?
Kein Mittel gäb's, das ihm gedieh'?
Sang er so schlecht, so fehlervoll,
dass nichts mehr zum Meister ihm
    helfen soll?

SACHS

Mein Kind, für den ist Alles verloren,
und Meister wird der in keinem Land;
denn wer als Meister ward geboren,
der hat unter Meistern den schlimmsten
    Stand.

MAGDALENE

Der Vater verlangt.

EVA

So sagt mir noch an,
ob keinen der Meister zum Freund er
    gewann?

SACHS

Das wär' nicht übel, Freund ihm noch
    sein!
Ihm, vor dem sich alle fühlten so klein?
Den Junker Hochmut, lasst ihn laufen!
Mag er durch die Welt sich raufen;
was wir erlernt mit Not und Müh',
dabei lasst uns in Ruh' verschnaufen,
hier renn' er uns nichts über'n Haufen,
sein Glück ihm anderswo erblüh'!

EVA (erhebt sich)

Ja, anderswo soll's ihm erblüh'n,
als bei euch garst'gen, neid'schen
    Mannsen;
wo warm die Herzen noch erglüh'n
trotz allen tück'schen Meister Hansen!
Gleich, Lene, gleich! Ich komme schon!
Was trüg' ich hier für Trost davon?
Da riecht's nach Pech, dass Gott
    erbarm'!
Brennt' er's lieber, da würd' er doch
    warm.

SACHS

Das dacht' ich wohl. Nun heisst's:
    schaff' Rat!

(*Er ist während des Folgenden damit
    beschäftigt, auch die obere Laden-
    türe so weit zu schliessen, dass sie nur
    ein wenig Licht noch durchlässt: er
    selbst verschwindet so fast ganz.*)

MAGDALENE

Hilf Gott! was bliebst du nur so spat?
Der Vater rief.

EVA

Geh' zu ihm ein:
ich sei zu Bett im Kämmerlein.

MAGDALENE

Nicht doch, hör' mich! Komm' ich
    dazu?
Beckmesser fand mich, er lässt nicht
    Ruh':
zur Nacht sollst du dich an's Fenster
    neigen,
er will dir 'was Schönes singen und
    geigen,
mit dem er dich hofft zu gewinnen, das
    Lied,
ob das dir nach Gefallen geriet.

EVA

Das fehlte auch noch! Käme nur Er!

MAGDALENE

Hast' David geseh'n?

EVA

Was soll mir der?

MAGDALENE (*für sich*)

Ich war zu streng; er wird sich grämen.

EVA

Siehst du noch nichts?

MAGDALENE

's ist als ob Leut' dort kämen.

EVA

Wär' er's!

MAGDALENE

Mach' und komm jetzt hinan!

EVA

Nicht eh'r, bis ich sah den teuersten
    Mann!

MAGDALENE

Ich täuschte mich dort: er war es nicht.
Jetzt komm, sonst merkt der Vater die
    Geschicht'!

EVA

Ach! meine Angst!

MAGDALENE

Auch lass uns beraten,
wie wir des Beckmesser's uns entladen.

EVA

Zum Fenster gehst du für mich.

MAGDALENE

Wie? Ich?
Das machte wohl David eiferlich?
Er schläft nach der Gassen: hihi! 'S wär
    fein!

EVA

Da hör' ich Schritte.

EVA

There's no hope left? Why?
Won't he be granted one more try?
Was he so bad, so much to blame,
that he must be barred from the master name?

SACHS

My child, that man was made for disaster,
nor master will be in any clime;
he who was born as a master
will have among masters the hardest time.

MAGDALENE

Your father has called.

EVA

This can't be the end;
did none of the masters speak up as his friend?

SACHS

You can't be serious. Friend we should
call him? the man who made us all
feel so small?
The haughty noble! Let him wander!
Let him roam both here and yonder.
What we have learned in many a year,
the rules of which we've grown ever fonder
we will not let him tear asunder.
We wish him happiness, but not here.

EVA (*rises angrily*)

Yes, somewhere else his luck will smile,
where no one's envy spoils his chances,
where hearts are warm and know no guile,
despite all nasty Master Hanses!
Yes, Lene, yes! I'm coming, now.
For all the help I'm getting here!
It smells of pitch! A crying shame!
Let him burn it and bask in the flame!

SACHS

I thought as much. Now Sachs, to work!

(*During the following he closes the upper half of the door so far that only a little light passes out: he himself disappears almost entirely.*)

MAGDALENE

Dear Lord! My child, where have you been?
Your father called!

EVA

Don't worry so,
I went to bed a while ago.

MAGDALENE

No! no! Listen! Only a word.
Beckmesser saw me; he will be heard.
Tonight, if only he can persuade you,
with fiddling and singing he'll serenade you;
you come to the window when all others rest;
tomorrow's song he'll put to the test.

EVA

That's all I need now. Where can he be?

MAGDALENE

Has David been here?

EVA

What's that to me?

MAGDALENE

I was too strict; I'm sure he's moping.

EVA

What do you see?

MAGDALENE

I see a shadow groping.

EVA

Stolzing!

MAGDALENE

Come! enough is enough!

EVA

Not yet!
I must see the one whom I love!

MAGDALENE

I must have been wrong. Not a soul about.
Now come, or else your father will find out.

EVA

I'm so afraid!

MAGDALENE

Let's try to discover
how to lose Beckmesser as a lover!

EVA

It's you who will take my place!

MAGDALENE

What? I? I'd like to see David's jealous face!
His room faces your room—hi-hi! What fun!

EVA

I hear a footstep.

MAGDALENE

Jetzt komm', es muss sein.

EVA

Jetzt näher!

MAGDALENE

Du irrst, ist nichts, ich wett.
Ei, komm! Du musst, bis der Vater zu
Bett.

POGNER (*von innen*)

He! Lene! Eva!

MAGDALENE

's ist höchste Zeit!
Hörst du's? Komm'! Dein Ritter ist
weit.

(*Walther ist die Gasse heraufgekommen; Eva reisst sich los und stürzt Walther entgegen.*)

EVA

Da ist er!

MAGDALENE (*hineingehend*)

Da haben wir's! Nun heisst's: gescheit!

EVA (*ausser sich*)

Ja, ihr seid es!
Nein! Du bist es!
Alles sag' ich,
denn ihr wisst es;
Alles klag' ich,
denn ich weiss es;
ihr seid beides,
Held des Preises,
und mein einz'ger Freund!

WALTHER

Ach, du irrst, bin nur dein Freund,
doch des Preises noch nicht würdig,
nicht den Meistern ebenbürtig:
mein Begeistern fand Verachten,
und ich weiss es, darf nicht trachten
nach der Freundin Hand!

EVA

Wie du irrst! Der Freundin Hand,
erteilt nur sie den Preis,

wie deinen Mut ihr Herz erfand,
reicht sie nur dir das Reis.

WALTHER

Ach nein, du irrst! Der Freundin
Hand,
wär keinem sie erkoren,
wie sie des Vaters Wille band,
mir wär' sie doch verloren.
"Ein Meistersinger muss es sein:
nur wen ihr krönt, den darf sie frei'n!"
So sprach er festlich zu den Herrn,
kann nicht zurück, möcht' er auch
gern!
Das eben gab' mir Mut;
wie ungewohnt mir alles schien,
ich sang voll Lieb' und Glut,
dass ich den Meisterschlag verdien'.
Doch diese Meister!
Ha, diese Meister!
Dieser Reimgesetzen
Leimen und Kleister!
Mir schwillt die Galle,
das Herz mir stockt,
denk' ich der Falle,
darein ich gelockt!
Fort in die Freiheit!
Dorthin gehör ich,
dort wo ich Meister im Haus.
Soll ich dich frei'n heut',
dich nun beschwör ich,
flieh' und folg' mir hinaus!
Nichts steht zu hoffen;
keine Wahl ist offen!
Überall Meister,
wie böse Geister,
seh' ich sich rotten,
mich zu verspotten,
mit den Gewerken,
aus den Gemerken,
aus allen Ecken,
auf allen Flecken,
seh' ich zu Haufen
Meister nur laufen,
mit höhnendem Nicken
frech auf dich blicken,
in Kreisen und Ringeln
dich zu umzingeln,
näselnd und kreischend
zur Braut dich heischend,
als Meisterbuhle
auf dem Singstuhle
zitternd und bebend,
hoch dich erhebend!
Und ich ertrüg' es, sollt' es nicht
wagen,
g'radaus tüchtig d'rein zu schlagen?
(*Man hört den starken Ruf eines Nachtwächterhornes.*)

MAGDALENE

Enough! Now come on.

EVA

He's coming!

MAGDALENE

You're wrong. He's not, I bet.
Now come. It's late, and your father
will fret.

POGNER

(from the interior)

He! Lene! Eva!

MAGDALENE

You mustn't stay!
Evchen—come! Your knight's far
away!

(Walther has come up the alley. Eva
tears herself away from Magdalene
and rushes toward Walther.)

EVA

I see him!

MAGDALENE

(going hastily into the house)

We're in for it! And now, watch out!

EVA

(beside herself)

Yes, my Stolzing! No, my Walther!
When I'm near you,
I don't falter;
when I'm near you,
doubt must flee me:
you will win me,
you will free me,
you, my only friend!

WALTHER

No, you're wrong: I am your friend,
yet unworthy
of their prizes,
one no master
recognizes.
They derided
my ambition.
Gone forever
is the vision
I might win your hand!

EVA

'Tis not so! If choose I may
to whom the prize is due,

since to my heart you found a way,
none shall be crowned but you!

WALTHER

Ah, no! You're wrong! This lovely
hand
you may keep on refusing,
yet by your father's own command
I am condemned to losing.
"A Mastersinger he must be!
One you crown, to wed she's free!"
That's what he said in solemn voice.
He can't go back, there is no choice.
That ruling made me strong;
though very strange was all I saw,
with love I filled my song,
to earn the mastername by law.
Ah! But those masters!
Ha! Those masters!
With their rhyming laws
of glue and plaster!
My heart stops beating!
I can't forget
how they deceived me,
the traps they have set!
No! Give me freedom!
There is my homeland
where I am master and free.
If you would wed me,
do hear my pleading,
come, together we flee!
I'm doomed to losing.
There can be no choosing!
Everywhere masters,
like dread disasters,
gathering beside me,
set to deride me!
Spying and harking,
viciously marking,
from every angle
I see them dangle,
staring and starting,
masters are darting,
with mocking advances
throwing you glances!
In circles around you
how they hound you!
Screeching and cooing,
they do their wooing:
the masters' wench
there on the singer's bench,
trembling and shameless,
calling you blameless.
And I should bear it? If I can't sway
them,
let me take my sword and slay them!

(The loud horn of the Nightwatchman is heard.)

EVA
(*fasst ihn besänftigend bei der Hand*)
Geliebter, spare den Zorn;
's war nur des Nachtwächters Horn.
Unter der Linde
birg' dich geschwinde:
hier kommt der Wächter vorbei.

MAGDALENE (*an der Türe, leise*)
Evchen! 's ist Zeit! mach' dich frei!

WALTHER
Du fliehst?

EVA
Muss ich denn nicht?

WALTHER
Entweichst?

EVA
Dem Meistergericht.
(*Sie verschwindet mit Magdalene im Hause.*)

DER NACHTWÄCHTER
Hört ihr Leut' und lasst euch sagen,
die Glock' hat Zehn geschlagen:
bewahrt das Feuer und auch das Licht,
damit Niemand kein Schad' geschicht.
Lobet Gott den Herrn!

SACHS
Üble Dinge, die ich da merk':
eine Entführung gar im Werk!
Aufgepasst! Das darf nicht sein.

WALTHER (*hinter der Linde*)
Käm' sie nicht wieder? O der Pein!
Doch ja! sie kommt dort! Weh' mir,
nein!
Die Alte ist's! Doch aber—ja!

EVA
(*ist in Magdalene's Kleidung wieder
zurückgekommen*)
Das tör'ge Kind: da hast du's, da!

WALTHER
O Himmel! Ja! nun wohl ich weiss,
dass ich gewann den Meisterpreis!

EVA
Doch nun kein Besinnen!
Von hinnen! Von hinnen!
O wären wir weit schon fort!

WALTHER
Hier durch die Gasse: dort
finden wir vor dem Tor
Knecht und Rosse vor.
(*Als sich Beide wenden, um in die
Gasse einzubiegen, lässt Sachs, nachdem er die Lampe hinter eine Glas-
kugel gestellt, einen hellen Licht-
schein durch die ganz wieder geöff-
nete Ladentüre quer über die Strasse
fallen, so dass Eva und Walther sich
plötzlich hell beleuchtet sehen.*)

EVA
(*Walther hastig zurückziehend*)
O weh', der Schuster! Wenn der uns
säh'!
Birg' dich, komm' ihm nicht in die
Näh'!

WALTHER
Welch' andrer Weg führt uns hinaus?

EVA
Dort durch die Strasse: doch der ist
kraus,
ich kenn' ihn nicht gut; auch stiessen
wir dort auf den Wächter.

WALTHER
Nun denn durch die Gasse.

EVA
Der Schuster muss erst vom Fenster
fort.

WALTHER
Ich zwing' ihn, dass er's verlasse.

EVA
Zeig' dich ihm nicht: er kennt dich.

WALTHER
Der Schuster?

EVA
's ist Sachs.

WALTHER
Hans Sachs? Mein Freund?

EVA
Glaub's nicht!
Von dir Übles zu sagen nur wusst' er.

WALTHER
Wie? Sachs? Auch er? Ich lösch' ihm
das Licht!
(*Beckmesser ist die Gasse heraufgekommen. Jetzt stimmt er eine mitge-
brachte Laute.*)

EVA
Tu's nicht! Doch horch!

WALTHER
Einer Laute Klang.

EVA

(*takes his hand soothingly*)
Beloved, master your scorn;
that was the nightwatchman's horn.
Hide in the shadow
under the tree there;
he'll see you if you should stay.

MAGDALENE

(*calls softly from the door*)
Evchen! It's late! Come away!

WALTHER

You'd leave?

EVA

Must I not flee?

WALTHER

From what?

EVA

The masters' decree!
(*She disappears with Magdalene into
the house.*)

NIGHTWATCHMAN

Listen to my words, good people,
it's ten o'clock on the steeple.
Now guard your fire and guard your
   light,
that no one is harmed tonight.
Praise be God, the Lord! (*goes off*)

SACHS

Evil things I notice at hand;
it's an elopement that is planned?
Careful now; that must not be!

WALTHER (*behind the linden tree*)
Could she desert me? Would she flee?
But no, she's right there! Worse luck:
   it's
the other one! Yet . . . it is . . . yes!

EVA

(*in Magdalene's dress, comes out of the
house*)
The foolish child, she's yours now!
There!

WALTHER

Beloved, in your lovely eyes
I see I've won the master prize!

EVA

There's no time to tarry!
Let's hurry; let's hurry;
and soon be far away!

WALTHER

Here, isn't this the way
leading us to the gate
where my horses wait?

(*As they both turn to go into the alley,
Sachs, after placing his lamp behind
a glass globe, lets a bright beam of
light fall across the alley through the
opened shutter so that Eva and Walther suddenly find themselves clearly
illuminated.*)

EVA

EVA (*hastily drawing Walther back*)
Good Lord, the cobbler! That is his
   light!
Hide here! Keep well out of his sight!

WALTHER

Which other road might lead us out?

EVA

There is a back street; it's roundabout,
I don't know it well, and there we
   might run into the watchman!

WALTHER

Well then, let's go this way!

EVA

But first the cobbler must leave his
   post!

WALTHER

He'd better, or else I'll make him!

EVA

Don't show your face; he knows you!

WALTHER

The cobbler?

EVA

'Tis Sachs!

WALTHER

Hans Sachs? My friend!

EVA

Your friend?
He said nothing but bad things about
   you!

WALTHER

What? Sachs? He, too? I'll put out
   his light!
(*Beckmesser has come up the alley. He
now tunes a lute he has brought.*)

EVA

No, don't! What's that?

WALTHER

It's a lute I hear.

EVA

Ach, meine Not!

WALTHER

Wie, wird dir bang?
Der Schuster, sieh, zog ein das Licht:
so sei's gewagt!

EVA

Weh'! Siehst du denn nicht?
Ein and'rer kam, und nahm dort
Stand.

WALTHER

Ich hör's und seh's: ein Musikant.
Was will der hier so spät des Nachts?

EVA

'S ist Beckmesser schon!

SACHS

Aha! ich dacht's!

WALTHER

Der Merker? Er in meiner Gewalt?
Drauf zu! Den Lung'rer mach' ich kalt.

EVA

Um Gott! So hör'! Willst den Vater
wecken?
Er singt ein Lied, dann zieht er ab.
Lass dort uns im Gebüsch verstecken.
Was mit den Männern ich Müh' doch
hab!

(Sie zieht Walther hinter das Gebüsch
auf die Bank unter der Linde. Beckmesser klimpert voll Ungeduld heftig
auf der Laute. Als er endlich anfan-
gen will zu singen, beginnt Sachs
laut mit dem Hammer auf den
Leisten zu schlagen.)

SACHS (sehr stark)

Jerum! Jerum!
Halla hallo!
Oho! Tralalei! Oho!
Als Eva aus dem Paradies
von Gott dem Herrn verstossen,
gar schuf ihr Schmerz der harte Kies
an ihrem Fuss, dem blossen.
Das jammerte den Herrn,
ihr Füsschen hatt' er gern,
und seinem Engel rief er zu:
da mach' der armen Sünd'rin Schuh';
und da der Adam, wie ich seh',
an Steinen dort sich stösst die Zeh',
das recht fortan
er wandeln kann,
so miss' dem auch Stiefeln an!

WALTHER (zu Eva)

Wie heisst das Lied? Wie nennt er
dich?

EVA

Ich hört' es schon: 's geht nicht auf
mich.
Doch eine Bosheit steckt darin.

WALTHER

Welch Zögernis! Die Zeit geht hin!

BECKMESSER

Was soll das sein?
Verdammtes Schrein!
Was fällt dem groben Schuster ein?
Wie, Meister? Auf? noch so spät zur
Nacht?

SACHS

Herr Stadtschreiber! Was, ihr wacht?
Die Schuh machen euch grosse Sorgen?
Ihr seht, ich bin dran: Ihr habt sie
morgen.

BECKMESSER (zornig)

Hol' der Teufel die Schuh'!
Hier will ich Ruh'!

SACHS

Jerum! Hal-la-hal-lo-he!
Oho! Tra-la-lei! Tra-la-lei!
O he! O Eva! Eva! Schlimmes Weib,
das hast du am Gewissen,
dass ob der Füss' am Menschenleib
jetzt Engel schustern müssen!

EVA

O Weh', der Pein!
Mir ahnt nichts Gutes.

WALTHER

Mein süsser Engel, sei guten Mutes!

SACHS

Bliebst du im Paradies,
da gab es keinen Kies';
um deiner jungen Missetat
hantier' ich jetzt mit Ahl' und Draht,
und ob Herrn Adam's übler Schwäch'
versohl' ich Schuh' and streiche Pech!
Wär' ich nicht fein ein Engel rein,
Teufel möchte Schuster sein! Je . . .

BECKMESSER

Gleich höret auf! Spielt ihr mir
Streich'?
Bleibt ihr Tag's und Nacht's euch
gleich?

SACHS

Wenn ich hier sing' was kümmert's
euch?
Die Schuhe sollen doch fertig werden?

BECKMESSER

So schliesst euch ein, und schweigt dazu
still!

EVA

Ah! I'm afraid!

WALTHER

What's there to fear?
The cobbler, look, put out his light.
Let's lose no time.

EVA

Wait, back out of sight!
Another came, he means to stay.

WALTHER

A man, a lute! He means to play?
What can he want so late at night?

EVA

'Tis Beckmesser, look!

SACHS

Aha! I'm right!

WALTHER

The marker? He? And here in my
    grasp?
That's good! He'll heave his final gasp!

EVA

Oh Lord, be still! You want to wake
    my father?
He'll sing a song; that will be fast.
Let's go and hide behind those bushes.
When will those menfolk grow up at
    last?
(She draws Walther onto the seat be-
hind the foliage under the linden tree.
Beckmesser strums impatiently on the
lute. When he at length prepares to
sing, Sachs strikes a heavy blow with
his hammer on the last.)

SACHS (very loud)

Jerum! Jerum!
Halla hallo he!
Oho! Tralalei! Oho!
When Eva was from Paradise
by God, our Lord, evicted,
her bare foot caused her many sighs,
when stones and pebbles kicked it.
That filled our Lord with woe;
her feet he cherished so.
His favorite angel he did choose
to make for her a pair of shoes,
and since poor Adam, as I know,
against those stones oft stubs his toe,
to make him walk without a care,
measure him another pair!

WALTHER (to Eva)

What is this song? He used your name.

EVA

I heard it, too. It's not the same.
Yet there's some malice in his rhyme.

WALTHER

We cannot wait! We're losing time!

BECKMESSER

What is this brawl?
Who dares to bawl?
The vulgar cobbler gets my gall!
You? Working? Now? But for heaven's
    sake!

SACHS

Herr Beckmesser! You awake?
Your shoes give you a lot of sorrow.
But look: they'll be done by dawn to-
    morrow!

BECKMESSER (angry)

Make the shoes when you will!
Only be still!

SACHS

Jerum! Halla Hallo he!
Oho! Tralalei! Tralalei!
Ohe! Oh Eva, Eva, worst of shrews,
it all has been your doing,
because your sinning feet wore shoes,
now angels do the shoeing!

EVA

I'm so afraid!
It's all so frightening.

WALTHER

My sweetest angel, you must have cour-
    age!

SACHS

Had you left fruit alone,
you'd never tread on stone,
Because you followed your giddy head,
I now sit here with awl and thread,
for Adam listened to that witch,
that's why I'm soling shoes with pitch!
If I were not like angels true,
devils only would make a shoe! Je—

BECKMESSER

That is enough! What is your game?
Day and night you are the same!

SACHS

I sing my song. Am I to blame?
Remember: you want these shoes by
    morning!

BECKMESSER

Then go inside and spare us your song.

SACHS

Des Nacht's arbeiten macht Beschwerden;
wenn ich da munter bleiben will,
so brauch' ich Luft und frischen Gesang:
drum hört, wie der dritte Vers gelang!

BECKMESSER

Er macht mich rasend! Das grobe Geschrei!
Am End' denkt sie gar, dass ich das sei!

SACHS

Jerum! Jerum!
O Eva! Hör' mein Klageruf,
mein' Not und schwer Verdrüssen!
Die Kunstwerk', die ein Schuster schuf,
sie tritt die Welt mit Füssen!
Gäb nicht ein Engel Trost,
der gleiches Werk erlos't,
und rief mich oft in's Paradies,
wie ich da Schuh' und Stiefel liess'!
Doch wenn der mich im Himmel hält,
dann liegt zu Füssen mir die Welt,
und bin in Ruh'
Hans Sachs ein Schuhmacher und Poet dazu.

BECKMESSER

Das Fenster geht auf: Herr Gott! 'S ist sie!

EVA

Mich schmerzt das Lied, ich weiss nicht wie!
O fort, lass' uns fliehen!

WALTHER

Nun denn: mit dem Schwert!

EVA

Nicht doch! Ach halt!

WALTHER

Kaum wär' er's wert!

EVA

Ja, besser Geduld! O lieber Mann!
Dass ich so Not dir machen kann!

WALTHER

Wer ist am Fenster?

EVA

's ist Magdalene.

WALTHER

Das heiss' ich vergelten. Fast muss ich lachen.

EVA

Wie ich ein End' und Flucht mir ersehne!

WALTHER

Ich wünscht', er möchte den Anfang machen.

BECKMESSER

Jetzt bin ich verloren, singt er noch fort!
Freund Sachs! So hört doch nur ein Wort!
Wie seid ihr auf die Schuh' versessen!
Ich hatt' sie wahrlich schon vergessen.
Als Schuster seid ihr mir wohl wert,
als Kunstfreund doch weit mehr verehrt.
Eu'r Urteil, glaubt, das halt' ich hoch;
d'rum bitt' ich: hört das Liedlein doch,
mit dem ich morgen möcht' gewinnen,
ob das auch recht nach euren Sinnen.

SACHS

Oha! Wollt mich beim Wahne fassen?
Mag mich nicht wieder schelten lassen.
Seit sich der Schuster dünkt Poet
gar übel es um euer Schuhwerk steht:
ich seh', wie's schlappt und überall klappt;
d'rum lass ich Vers und Reim'
gar billig nun daheim,
Verstand und Witz, und Kenntnis dazu
mach' euch für morgen die neuen Schuh'!

BECKMESSER

Lasst das doch sein! Das war ja nur Scherz,
Vernehmt besser wie's mir ums Herz.
Vom Volk seid ihr geehrt,
auch der Pognerin seid ihr wert:
will ich vor aller Welt
nun morgen um die werben,
sagt! könnt's mich nicht verderben,
wenn mein Lied euch nicht gefällt?
D'rum hört mich ruhig an,
und sang ich, sagt mir dann,
was euch gefällt, was nicht,
dass ich mich darnach richt'!

SACHS

Ei lasst mich doch in Ruh'!
Wie käm' solche Ehr' mir zu?
Nur Gassenhauer dicht' ich zum meisten:
D'rum sing' ich zur Gassen, und hau' auf den Leisten!
Jerum! Jerum!
Hallo-hallo-he!

BECKMESSER

Verfluchter Kerl! Den Verstand verlier' ich,
mir seinem Lied voll Pech und Schmierich!
Schweigt doch! Weckt ihr die Nachbarn auf?

SACHS

This poor shoemaker feels like yawning;
if I'm to work the whole night through,
I need fresh air; some music to cheer:
so now it's the final verse you'll hear!
Jerum! Jerum!

BECKMESSER

I'll lose my mind yet! How coarse every
   word!
She might think that it was I she
   heard!

SACHS

Oh, Eva! Hear my wounded heart,
my tale of woe is ample;
the cobbler makes a work of art
on which the world will trample!
But for an angel above
who's making shoes for love,
and often calls me to heaven's throne,
I'd soon leave boots and shoes alone!
But when he holds me in the sky,
then at my feet the world goes by,
and peace is due
Hans Sachs, a shoe-
maker and a poet too!

BECKMESSER

The window has moved! Good God!
   It's she!

EVA

That song has hurt me, why should that
   be?
Away! Let us hurry!

WALTHER

You're right! To the gates!

EVA

Ah, no! Not that!

WALTHER

It's more than he rates.

EVA

I think we should wait. I love you so;
why must I bring you only woe?

WALTHER

Who's at the window?

EVA

It's Magdalene.

WALTHER

He gets his comeuppance! I can't help
   laughing!

EVA

Oh, how I wish it all would be over.

WALTHER

I wonder why he has not begun yet.

BECKMESSER

If he goes on singing, I am undone!
One word! before you're going on.
Why should my shoes be so much
   bother?
In that case I forget them, rather.
In cobbling I admire your skill;
as artist you are greater still.
Your judgment, Sachs, is never wrong;
and therefore hear my little song
with which I hope to win a treasure,
and tell me if it meets with your pleasure.

SACHS

Oh, no! Flattery will get you nowhere.
And tomorrow you'll start again scold-
   ing:
"why, since my shoemaker also makes
   verse,
for all his verses my shoes are worse.
You see, they snap; they wiggle and
   flap!"
Therefore to verse and rhyme
I'll give no more of my time,
conceits of mind and wits I'll eschew,
all I will do is make shoes for you!

BECKMESSER

Don't start again; 'twas only a jest.
I'll now tell you what's on my chest.
The people worship you;
Eva Pogner respects you too.
Before the festive throng tomorrow I'll
   be wooing;
why, 't would be my undoing
if Hans Sachs disliked my song.
So let me sing in peace,
and tell me, if you please,
what suits you more, what less;
so I can make redress.

SACHS

Ah, can't you let me be;
how could such honor come to me?
It's gutter couplets I put together;
I sing in the gutter and cobble the
   leather!
Jerum! Jerum! Hallo-hallo-he!

BECKMESSER

Accursed fool!
He disturbs my thinking!
Of tar and pitch his song is stinking!
Silence! You will awake the street!

SACHS
Die sind's gewöhnt, 's hört keiner
d'rauf.
"O Eva! Eva!" . . .

BECKMESSER
Oh, ihr boshafter Geselle!
Ihr spielt mir heut' den letzten Streich:
schweigt ihr jetzt nicht auf der Stelle,
so denkt ihr d'ran, das schwör' ich
euch.
Neidisch seid ihr, nichts weiter:
dünkt ihr euch auch gleich gescheiter;
dass and're auch was sind, ärgert euch
schändlich:
glaubt, ich kenne euch aus und in-
wendlich!
Dass man euch noch nicht zum
Merker gewählt,
das ist's was den gallischen Schuster
quält.
Nun gut! So lang als Beckmesser
lebt,
und ihm noch ein Reim an den Lippen
klebt;
so lang' ich noch bei den Meistern
was gelt',
ob Nürnberg blüh' und wachs',
das schwör' ich Herrn Hans Sachs,
nie wird er je zum Merker bestellt!

SACHS
War das eu'r Lied?

BECKMESSER
Der Teufel hol's!

SACHS
Zwar wenig Regel, doch klang's recht
stolz.

BECKMESSER
Wollt ihr mich hören?

SACHS
In Gottes Namen,
singt zu: ich schlag' auf die Sohl' die
Rahmen.

BECKMESSER
Doch schweigt ihr still?

SACHS
Ei, singet ihr, die Arbeit, schaut,
fördert's auch mir.

BECKMESSER
Das verfluchte Klopfen wollt ihr doch
lassen?

SACHS
Wie sollt' ich die Sohl' euch richtig
fassen?

BECKMESSER
Was? Ihr wollt klopfen, und ich soll
singen?

SACHS
Euch muss dass Lied, mir der Schuh
gelingen.

BECKMESSER
Ich mag keine Schuh'!

SACHS
Das sagt ihr jetzt:
in der Singschul' ihr mir's dann wieder
versetzt.
Doch hört! Vielleicht sich's richten
lässt;
zweieinig geht der Mensch am best'.
Darf ich die Arbeit nicht entfernen,
die Kunst des Merker's möcht' ich
erlernen;
darin kommt euch nun keiner gleich;
ich lern' sie nie, wenn nicht von euch.
D'rum singt ihr nun,
ich acht' und merk',
und fördr' auch wohl dabei mein Werk.

BECKMESSER
Merkt immer zu, und was nicht
gewann,
nehmt eure Kreide, und streicht mir's
an.

SACHS
Nein, Herr! Da fleckten die Schuh' mir
nicht:
mit dem Hammer auf den Leisten halt'
ich Gericht.

BECKMESSER
Verdammte Bosheit! Gott, und 'swird
spät!
Am End' mir die Jungfer vom Fenster
geht!
(Er klimpert wie um anzufangen.)

SACHS
Fanget an, 's pressiert: sonst sing' ich
für mich!

BECKMESSER
Haltet ein! Nur das nicht! (Teufel! wie
ärgerlich!)
Wollt ihr euch denn als Merker erdreisten,
nun gut, so merkt mit dem Hammer
auf den Leisten;
nur mit dem Beding, nach den Regeln
scharf,
aber nichts, was nach den Regeln ich
darf.

SACHS
Nach den Regeln, wie sie der Schuster
kennt,
dem die Arbeit unter den Händen
brennt.

BECKMESSER
Auf Meisterehr'?

SACHS
Und Schustermut!

BECKMESSER
Nicht einen Fehler; glatt und gut.

SACHS

They're used to it; they pay no heed,
Oh Eva, Eva, ...

BECKMESSER

Oh you scoundrel with a hammer!
Don't try to play another trick!
If you don't stop all that clamor,
you'll hear from me and very quick!
Envy plagues you; none greener!
You believe that you are keener.
That others also count irks you
  infernally.
Yes, I know you both ex- and internally.
That you've never been a marker at all,
that's what has been getting our cob-
  bler's gall!
But wait! As long as Beckmesser kicks,
and a single rhyme to his lips yet sticks,
as long as masters still pay respect,
however Nürnberg fare,
Hans Sachs, I hereby swear,
never shall be a marker elect!

SACHS

Was that your song?

BECKMESSER

Oh, go to sleep!

SACHS

A bit unruly, but very deep.

BECKMESSER

Now will you hear me?

SACHS

Well, if you have to, sing then;
and I will continue working.

BECKMESSER

You'll keep your peace?

SACHS

Come, sing your song,
I'll cobble as you go along.

BECKMESSER

But you won't continue hammering the
  leather?

SACHS

How else can I put your shoes together?

BECKMESSER

What of my singing? My inspiration?

SACHS

You care for songs, shoes are my
  preoccupation.

BECKMESSER

I don't want a shoe.

SACHS

That's only talk,
but in school you'll blame me if you
  cannot walk.
But wait:
a means may yet be found.
Agreement makes the world go 'round.
Though making shoes still is my
  mission,
to be a marker is my ambition.
And in that art you have no peer;
I'll learn it best right now and here.
You sing your song,
I mark each phrase,
and thus my work will go apace.

BECKMESSER

Go right ahead, and where you object,
reach for your chalk and mark each
  defect!

SACHS

No, no, your shoes would remain un-
  soled.
With my hammer on the last I'll mark
  every fault.

BECKMESSER (strumming eagerly)

He's full of malice! my, it is late!
Who knows how much longer the girl
  will wait?

SACHS

Let's begin! Don't wait, or I'll start to
  sing!

BECKMESSER

Don't you dare! Be quiet! (Devil! How
  maddening!)
You dare attempt the marker's profes-
  sion?
Agreed, but then use your hammer with
  discretion.
And do not forget, rigid rules prevail.
Understand? Only by rules can I fail.

SACHS

Do not worry, I shall obey the rules,
as a cobbler who wants to use his tools.

BECKMESSER

A master's word?

SACHS

A cobbler's oath!

BECKMESSER

Nothing to censure, smooth and neat.

SACHS
Dann ging't ihr morgen unbeschuht.
Setzt euch denn hier!

BECKMESSER
Lasst hier mich stehen.

SACHS
Warum so weit?

BECKMESSER
Euch nicht zu sehen,
wie's Brauch in der Schul' vor dem Gemerk!

SACHS
Da hör' ich euch schlecht.

BECKMESSER
Der Stimme Stärk'
ich so gar lieblich dämpfen kann.

SACHS
(Wie fein!) Nun gut denn! Fanget an!

WALTHER (zu Eva)
Welch' toller Spuck! Mich dünkt's ein
Traum:
den Singstuhl, scheint's, verliess ich
kaum!

EVA
Die Schläf' umwebt mir's wie ein
Wahn:
ob's Heil, ob Unheil, was ich ahn'?

BECKMESSER (zur Laute)
"Den Tag seh' ich erscheinen,
der mir wohl gefall'n tut . . .
(Sachs schlägt auf.
Beckmesser zuckt, fährt aber fort.)
"Da fasst mein Herz sich einen
guten und frischen"—
(Sachs hat zweimal aufgeschlagen.)
Treibt ihr hier Scherz?
Was wär' nicht gelungen?

SACHS
Besser gesungen:
"da fasst mein Herz
sich einen guten und frischen"?

BECKMESSER
Wie soll sich das reimen
auf "seh' ich erscheinen?"

SACHS
Ist euch an der Weise nichts gelegen?
Mich dünkt, sollt' passen Ton und
Wort.

BECKMESSER
Mit euch zu streiten? Lasst von den
Schlägen,
sonst denkt ihr mir dran!

SACHS
Jetzt fahret fort!

BECKMESSER
Bin ganz verwirrt!

SACHS
So fangt noch 'mal an:
drei Schläg' ich jetzt pausieren kann.

BECKMESSER (für sich)
Am besten, wenn ich ihn gar nicht be-
acht':
wenn's nur die Jungfer nicht irre
macht!
(Er beginnt wieder.)
"Den Tag seh' ich erscheinen,
der mir wohl gefall'n tut;
das fasst mein Herz sich einen
guten und frischen Mut.
Da denk' ich nicht an Sterben,
lieber an Werben
um jung Mägdelein's Hand.
Warum wohl aller Tage
schönster mag dieser sein?
Allen hier ich es sage:
weil ein schönes Fräulein
von ihrem lieb'n Herrn Vater,
wie gelobt hat er,
ist bestimmt zum Eh'stand.
Wer sich getrau',
der komm' und schau'
dasteh'n die hold lieblich Jungfrau,
auf die ich all' mein Hoffnung bau':
darum ist der Tag so schön blau,
als ich anfänglich fand."
(Er bricht wütend um die Ecke auf
Sachs los.)
Sachs! Seht, ihr bringt mich um!
Wollt ihr jetzt schweigen?

SACHS
Ich bin ja stumm!
Die Zeichen merk' ich; wir sprechen
dann;
derweil' lassen die Sohlen sich an.

BECKMESSER
Sie entweicht. Bst! Bst! Herr Gott, ich
muss!
Sachs, euch gedenk' ich die Ärgernuss.

SACHS
Merker am Ort: fahret fort!

BECKMESSER
"Will heut' mir das Herz hüpfen,
werben um Fräulein jung,
doch tät' der Vater knüpfen
daran ein Bedingung
für den, der ihn beerben
will und auch werben
um sein Kindelein fein.
Der Zunft ein bied'rer Meister,

SACHS

And then tomorrow, naked feet!
Sit down, my friend.

BECKMESSER

I'll stay behind you.

SACHS

So far away?

BECKMESSER

I must not see you.
The marker hides, thus it was ruled.

SACHS

But how shall I hear?

BECKMESSER

My voice is schooled
to start at will; now thick, now thin.

SACHS

(How smart!) I'm ready! Now begin!

WALTHER (*to Eva*)

It's like a dream. . . . That silly fool!
Am I still on the singer's stool?

EVA

The night has grazed me with its spell.
It's good or bad luck, I can't tell.

BECKMESSER

(*accompanying himself on the lute*)

The day I see appearing
that so much delights me,
       (*Sachs strikes.*)
it fills my heart with cheering
thoughts and happy. . . .
       (*Sachs strikes twice.*)
Is this a joke?
What's not by the letter?

SACHS

It would be better:
"It fills my heart
with cheering thoughts and happy."

BECKMESSER

And may I please ask how that
rhymes with "appearing"?

SACHS

You think that the music does not
    matter?
I thought that words and tune were
    one.

BECKMESSER

I will not argue. Stop all that clatter,
or else you will see.

SACHS

Well, let's go on!

BECKMESSER

I'm all confused.

SACHS

Then start it once more;
I'll skip the knocks I marked before.

BECKMESSER (*aside*)

I'll simply act as if he were not there.
If only Eva does not despair!

The day I see appearing
that so much delights me.
It fills my heart with cheering
thoughts and with happy glee.
I do not think of dying,
rather of vying
for a lovely young thing.
Why is this day, you ponder,
most enchanting to men?
I'll reply if you wonder,
it's because a maiden,
as her father dear chose it,
(everyone knows it)
must prepare her wedding.
You'd think so, too,
if you but knew
this virgin of purest virtue,
whom I so dearly hope to woo,
and that's why this day appears blue,
of which I gaily sing.
(*He springs forward in a rage.*)
Sachs! Please, you make me choke.
    Won't you keep quiet?

SACHS

I never spoke!
I did my marking. No time to lose.
Right now, let me put soles on your
    shoes.

BECKMESSER

Is she gone? Psst! Psst! No more delays.
Sachs, I'll remember your wicked ways.

SACHS

Markers don't rest. On with the test!

BECKMESSER

The joy makes my heart merry,
courting the fairest one,
despite her father's very
difficult condition
for him who would inherit
his gold and merit
that child without a flaw.
A master, wise and knowing,

wohl sein' Tochter er liebt,
doch zugleich auch beweis't er,
was er auf die Kunst gibt:
zum Preise muss es bringen
im Meistersingen,
wer sein Eidam will sein.
Nun gilt es Kunst,
dass mit Vergunst,
ohn' all' schädlich gemeinen Dunst
ihm glücke des Preises Gewunst,
wer begehrt mit wahrer Inbrunst
um die Jungfrau zu frei'n."

SACHS
Seid ihr nun fertig?

BECKMESSER (*in höchster Angst*)
Wie fraget ihr?

SACHS
(*die Schuhe triumphierend heraus-
haltend*)
Mit den Schuhen ward ich fertig
schier.
Das heiss' ich mir echte Merkerschuh':
mein Merkersprüchlein hört dazu!
Mit lang' und kurzen Hieben
steht's auf der Sohl' geschrieben:
da lest es klar
und nehmt es wahr,
und merkt's euch immerdar.
Gut Lied will Takt,
wer den verzwackt,
dem Schreiber mit der Feder
haut ihn der Schuster auf's Leder.
Nun lauft in Ruh',
habt gute Schuh':
der Fuss euch drin nicht knackt:
ihn hält die Sohl' im Takt!

BECKMESSER
"Darf ich mich Meister nennen,
das bewähr' ich heut' gern,
weil ich nach dem Preis brennen
muss, dursten und hungern.
Nun ruf' ich die neun Musen
dass an sie blusen
mein dicht'rischen Verstand.
Wohl kenn' ich alle Regeln,
halte gut Maass und Zahl;
doch Sprung und Überkegeln
wohl passiert je einmal,
wann der Kopf ganz voll Zagen
zu frei'n will wagen
um jung Mägdelein's Hand.
Ein Junggesell
trug ich mein Fell,
mein Ehr', Amt, Würd' und Brot zur
Stell',
dass euch mein Gesang wohl gefäll',
und mich das Jungfräulein erwähl',
wann sie mein Lied gut fand."

DAVID
(*ist, mit einem Knüppel bewaffnet,
hinter dem Laden aus dem Fenster
hervorgesprungen.*)
Wer Teufel hier? Und drüben gar?
Die Lene ist's, ich seh' es klar!
Herr Je! Der war's, den hat sie
bestellt.
Der ist's, der ihr besser als ich gefällt.
Nun warte, du kriegst's! Dir streich'
ich das Fell!
Zum Teufel mit dir verdammter Kerl!

MAGDALENE
Ach Himmel! David! Gott, welche
Not!
Zu Hilfe! zu Hilfe! Sie schlagen sich
tot.

BECKMESSER (*mit David sich balgend*)
Verfluchter Bursch! Lässt du mich los?

DAVID
Gewiss! Die Glieder brech' ich dir
bloss!
(*Sie balgen und prügeln sich in einem
fort.*)

NACHBARN
(*erst einige, dann immer mehrere
öffnen die Fenster und gucken
heraus.*)
Wer heult denn da? Wer kreischt mit
Macht?
Ist das erlaubt, so spät zur Nacht?
Gebt Ruhe hier! S'ist Schlafenszeit.
Mein', hört nur wie der Esel schreit!
Ihr da, seid still und schert euch fort!
Heult, kreischt und schreit an andrem
Ort!

Seht nach! Springt zu! Da würgen sich
zwei!
Heda! Herbei! 'S gibt Schlägerei!
Ihr da, lasst los, gebt freien Lauf!
Lasst ihr nicht los, wir schlagen drauf!

Ei, seht, auch ihr hier? Was sucht ihr
hier?
Geht's euch was an? Hat man euch
'was getan?
Euch kennt man gut! Euch noch viel
besser!
Wie so denn? Ei, so! Esel! Dummrian!
Wird euch wohl bange!
Euch gönnt' ich's schon lange!
Das für die Klage!
Seht euch vor wenn ich schlage!
Hat euch die Frau gehetzt?

a kind father at heart,
he insists now on showing
how much he adores art.
The prize you'll have to bring her
as mastersinger
to be his son-in-law.
Make no mistake!
It's for art's sake,
without harmful and vulgar fake.
He can win the prize that's at stake,
but his passion must not forsake
  if he wants to win her.

SACHS

Is this the end, now?

BECKMESSER (in anguish)

How do you dare?

SACHS

(holds out the completed shoes in
  triumph)
To your shoes I've given all my care,
and that's what I call a marker's shoe;
the marker's ditty is for you!
With hammer strokes I wrote it;
here on the sole it's noted.
Now come and read,
and pay it heed,
a lesson that you need.
Good song needs beat.
If that's not neat,
the faults of quill and feather
the cobbler knocks on his leather.
Do rest your mind.
Your shoes, you'll find,
now will not pinch your feet.
The sole will keep the beat!

BECKMESSER

To gain the master title
to all else I prefer;
of all it's the most vital
prize to still my hunger;
I call on the nine muses,
that each infuses
my mind with poetry.
I know the rules of thumb well,
no bar nor beat I skip;
sometimes I jump and tumble,
a permissible slip,
for it's fear that's distorting
one who is courting
a maid young and lovely.
A bachelor,
I set great store,
I risk pride, work, and bread, and
  more,

that you like my words and my score,
and that the maid I'm singing for
should at least favor me.

DAVID

(armed with a cudgel, comes back)
Now who is that? And this one here?
It's Lene, ha! It's very clear!
Good Lord! It's he! The woman is she!
It's he whom the wanton prefers to me!
Just give me a chance! I'll soften your
  hide!
The devil take your skin and curse your
  soul!

MAGDALENE

Oh heavens! David! Don't lose your
  head!
Come help them, and stop them! They
  both will be dead!

BECKMESSER

You wicked boy! Leave me alone!

DAVID

I will, but first I'll break all your bones!

NEIGHBORS

(First a few, then more and more open
  the windows on the alley and look
  out.)
Who's howling there? Who bleats like
  sheep?
Is this allowed, while I'm asleep?
Be quiet here! It's time for bed!
He's braying like a donkey's head!
Be still and disappear!
Yell and howl but please not here!
What's this? They cut each other's
  throat!
There is a fight; they scratch and bite.
Leave him alone! Why pick on him?
If not, we'll tear you limb from limb.
Surprise! Awake still! What do you
  want!
Why should you care? In your place,
  I'd beware!
We all know you! You even better!
And how so? Like this! Jackass! Dumb-
  head!
Your legs are shaking!
You've earned what you're getting!
Here! that will teach you!
You watch out when I reach you!
Your wife has egged you on!

Schaut, wie es Prügel setzt.
Lümmel! Grobian! Racker! Zwacker!
Seid ihr noch nicht gewitzt?
So schlagt doch! Das sitzt.
Dass dich Halunken gleich ein Don-
nerwetter träf'!
Wartet, ihr Racker,
Ihr Massabzwacker,
Wird euch bang?
Euch gönnt' ich's lang.

Wollt ihr noch mehr? Packt euch jetzt
heim,
Sonst kriegt ihr's von der Frau!
Geht's euch was an, wenn ich nicht
will?
Schickt die Gesellen heim!
So gut wie ihr bin Meister ich!
Macht euch fort! Dummer Kerl!
Schert euch heim! Haltet's Maul!
Schlagt sie nieder. Wir weichen nicht!
Immer 'ran! Wacker zu!
Schert euch fort und macht euch heim.
Alle Zünfte heraus!

NACHBARINNEN

Was ist das für Zanken und Streit?
Gleich auseinander da, ihr Leut'!
Da gibts gewiss noch Schlägerei?
Da ist mein Mann gewiss dabei!
Ach, welche Not! Mein', seht nur dort!
Der Zank und Lärm! Der Lärm und
Streit!
'S wird einem wahrlich angst und
bang.
Heda, ihr dort unten, so seid doch nur
gescheit!
Seit ihr denn alle gleich zu Streit und
Zank bereit?
Mein! Dort schlägt sich mein Mann.
Ach Gott, sah ich nur meinen Hans!
Ach! Sieht man die an? Seit ihr alle
denn toll?
Sind euch vom Wein die Köpfe voll?
Mein', dort den Michel seht, der haut
dem Steffen eins!
Seht dort den Christian, er walkt den
Peter ab!
Hilfe der Vater! Ach, sie hau'n ihn tot!
Jesus, sie schlagen meinen Jungen tot!
Jesus, der Hans hat einen Hieb am
Kopf!
Gott, wie sie walken, wie sie wackeln
hin und her!
Gott, welche Höllennot! Wer hört sein
eigen' Wort?
Hei! Mein Mann schlägt wacker auf
sie drein!

Die Köpf und Zöpfe wackeln hin und
her.

Wie soll das enden? Welches Toben,
welches Krachen!
Auf, schaffet Wasser her! Wasser ist
das allerbest' für ihre Wut.
Da giesst ihn' auf die Köpf' hinab!
Auf, schreit zu Hilfe: Mord und Zeter!
Hier an's Fenster! Bringt Wasser nur,
sonst schlagen sie sich tot!
Krug und Kanne, Topf und Hafen, alles
voll, und giesst's ihn' auf den Kopf!

LEHRLINGE

*(einzeln, dann mehr kommen von allen
Seiten.)*

Herbei, herbei! 'S gibt Keilerei!
'Sind die Schuster. Nein, 's sind die
Schneider!
Die Trunkenbolde, Hungerleider!
Kennt man die Schlosser nicht,
Die haben's sicher angericht'.
Ich glaub' die Schmiede werden's sein.
Nein, 'sind die Schlosser dort, ich wett'!
Ich kenn' die Schreiner dort!
Gewiss, die Metzger sind's.
Hei! Schaut die Schäffler dort beim
Tanz!
Dort seh' die Bader ich im Glanz.
Immer mehr! 'S gibt grosse Keilerei!
Krämer finden sich zur Hand
Mit Gerstenstang und Zuckerkand,
Mit Pfeffer, Zimmt, Muskatennuss,
sie riechen schön, doch machen viel
Verdruss,
und bleiben gern vom Schuss.
Meinst du damit etwa mich?
Halt's Maul! Hei, das sitzt!
Seht nur der Has',
Hat überall die Nas'.
Immer mehr heran,
Jetzt fängts erst richtig an.
Hei nun geht's! Plautz, hast du nicht
geseh'n!
Hast's auf der Schnautz! Ha! Nun
geht's: Krach!
Hagelwetterschlag! Pardautz!
Wo es sitzt da wächst nichts so bald
nach!
Jetzt fährt's hinein wie Hagelschlag!
Bald setzt es blut'ge Köpf', Arm' und
Bein'.
Dort der Pfister denkt daran.
Hei, der hat's, der hat genug!
Scher' sich jeder heim, wer nicht mit
keilt.

Here, take another one!
Fathead! Ruffian! Filcher! Bilker!
Perhaps you still want more!
I dare you! Galore!
I wished that lightning hit your addle-
    pated head!
You'll get a beating!
Always cheating!
Black and blue!
You got your due!
You want some more? Better go home;
    you'll get it from your wife.
What's it to you if I stay here?
Off with you journeymen!
Don't order me, I'm master, too!
Go away! Stupid fool!
You go home. Shut your mouth!
Knock their heads off! We don't give
    way!
Why don't you go home and get some
    sleep?
Cobblers, tanners, tinkers, bakers,
    weavers!
Grocers, butchers, joiners, locksmiths!
Come on.

NEIGHBORS (WOMEN)

What is all this brawling about?
It seems a fight's about to start!
I bet my husband will take part!
Ah! What a plight! Look over there!
The noisy fight, enough to make you
    sick!
Hey there, you below there, have you
    no sense at all?
What can you gain by all that fight
    and noise and brawl?
There I see my old man!
I wished I could see my own Hans!
Oh, my God, what a sight! You are all
    mad and blind!
Those silly heads are full of wine.
Lord, look at Michael there, he pounds
    poor Stephen's block!
There I see Christian, how he whacks
    poor Peter's back!
Help us! my husband, they will kill him
    yet!
Jesus, they're murdering my little boy!
Jesus, they put a hole in Hans's head!
Lord, how they hammer, how they wrig-
    gle to and fro!
Lord, do have mercy, make them end
    this awful fray!
Hey, my husband whacks a valiant
    blow!
Lord, what a night! I can't hear what I
    say.

Their heads and hair are shaking in the
    storm.
Ah, what will the end be? What an
    uproar! What a smash-up!
Quick, bring some water here! Water
    is the very best to drown their rage.
Now, let's pour it down on them!
Let's cry for help and let's cry murder;
    come here!
From the window! bring water here,
    they'll murder everyone!
Pots and pitchers, pail and bucket! fill
    them up and pour them on their
    heads!

PRENTICES

(come from all sides, first singly then in
numbers)

Come here! right now! we'll have a
    row!
Look, the cobblers! These are the
    tailors.
Those drunken fellows; and hunger-
    stricken!
Well, you may bet your life,
the locksmiths started all this strife;
I'm sure it is the locksmiths' fault!
Those are the locksmiths there, I bet!
I see the joiners there!
The butchers won't be far!
Are those the barbers there by chance?
Come on, come on, come to the dance!
Look at the coopers, how they dance!
More and more the battle grows and
    grows!
Chandlers we would never miss,
with candysticks and licorice,
with pepper, nuts and cinnamon.
They smell quite good but they are not
    much fun.
And when they fight, they run.
Do your words refer to me?
Shut up! What a blow!
Look at that bloke!
He has a nose to poke!
All of you come on!
It's time to start the fun!
How they hit! Smack! That's a sight to
    see!
Right on his snout! Here we go! One!
    Two!
Hail and thunderstorm!
Where we hit no grass will grow awhile!
The mighty blows like thunder claps.
We'll see some bloody heads, arms, and
    legs!
This he won't forget so soon!
What a hit! He had his share!
Everyone go home who does not fight!

Haltet selbst Gesellen mutig Stand.
Wer wich' s'wär wahrlich eine
    Schand'.
Immer mehr! Hei, Juchhe!
Immer lustig, nicht gewichen!
Wacker drauf und dran!
Wir stehen Alle wie ein Mann!

GESELLEN
(mit Knütteln bewaffnet, kommen von
    verschiedenen Seiten)
Heda Gesellen, 'ran!
Dort wird mit Zank und Streit getan,
Da gibt's gewiss noch Schlägerei:
Gesellen, haltet euch dabei!
'Sind die Weber! 'Sind die Gerber!
Die Preisverderber! Wischt's ihnen aus!
Gebt's denen scharf!
Dacht' ich mir's doch gleich:
Spielen immer Streich'.
Immer mehr, die Keilerei wird gross.
Dort den Metzger Klaus, kenn' ich
    heraus!
'S ist morgen der Fünfte.
'S brennt manchem im Haus!
Hei! Hier setzt's Prügel!
Schneider mit dem Bügel!
Zünfte heraus! Bald ist der Fünfte!
Nur tüchtig drauf und dran,
    wir schlagen los!
Ihr da macht! Packt euch fort!
Wir sind hier grad am Ort!
Wolltet ihr etwa den Weg uns hier
    verwehren?
Macht Platz! Wir schlagen drein!
Gürtler! Spengler! Zinngieser! Leim-
    sieder! Lichtsieder!
Schert euch selber fort
Wir sind grad am Ort!
Nicht gewichen! Tuchscherer! Lein-
    weber!
Immer 'ran, wer's noch wagt!
Immer drauf und dran!
Alle Zünfte heraus!

MEISTER UND ÄLTERE BÜRGER
Was gibt's denn da für Zank und
    Streit?
Das tost ja weit und breit.
Gebt Ruh' und schert nach Haus euch
    heim,
sonst schlag' ein Hageldonnerwetter
    d'rein.
Stemmt euch hier nicht mehr zu Hauf',
sonst schlagen wir Meister selbst noch
    drein!
Jetzt hilft nichts, Meister! Schlagt
    selbst d'rein!

MAGDALENE
Ach Himmel! Meine Not ist gross.

David! So hör' mich doch nur an!
So lass' doch nur den Herrn los!
Er hat mir nichts getan
'S ist Herr Beckmesser!

POGNER
(ist im Nachtgewand oben an das Fenster getreten.)
Um Gott! Eva! Schliess' zu!
Ich seh', ob im Haus unten Ruh'!

WALTHER
Jetzt gilt's zu wagen,
sich durchzuschlagen!
(Walther dringt mit geschwungenem
Schwerte bis in die Mitte der Bühne
vor, um sich mit Eva durch die Gasse
durchzuhauen. Da springt Sachs mit
einem kräftigen Satze aus dem Laden, bahnt sich mit geschwungenem
Knieriemen den Weg bis zu Walther
und packt diesen beim Arm.)

POGNER (auf der Treppe)
He! Lene! Wo bist du?

SACHS
(die halbohnmächtige Eva die Treppe
hinauf stossend)
In's Haus, Jungfer Lene!
(Pogner empfängt sie und zieht sie
beim Arme herein.)
(Sachs zieht Walther mit sich hinein
und schliesst hinter sich zu.)
(Lehrbuben, Bürger und Gesellen
suchen in eiliger Flucht sich nach
allen Seiten hin zu entfernen, so
dass die Bühne sehr schnell gänzlich
geleert ist.)

DER NACHTWAECHTER
Hört ihr Leut', und lasst euch sagen:
die Glock' hat Elfe geschlagen.
Bewahrt euch vor Gespenstern und
    Spuck,
dass kein böser Geist eu'r Seel' beruck'!
Lobet Gott den Herrn!
(Er geht langsam die Gasse hinab. Der
Vorhang fällt mit dem letzten Takt.)

DRITTER AUFZUG

In Sachsens Werkstatt. Im Hintergrunde die halbgeöffnete Ladentüre,
nach der Strasse führend. Rechts zur
Seite eine Kammertüre. Links das
nach der Gasse gehende Fenster, mit
Blumenstöcken davor, zur Seite ein
Werktisch. Sachs sitzt auf einem
grossen Lehnstuhle an diesem Fenster, durch welches die Morgensonne
hell auf ihn hereinscheint; er hat vor
sich auf dem Schosse einen grossen
Folianten, und ist im Lesen vertieft.

Never falter, show those fellows you are
   just as good!
Don't yield or you will be ashamed!
More and more! Hey! Yoo-hoo!
Merry fighters! No one budges!
Pounce with main and might!
We are all together in this fight.

JOURNEYMEN

(armed with clubs, come on from different sides)
Follow me one and all,
I think I hear a lovely brawl,
I'm sure a fight's about to start
and we, my friends, must all take part!
It's the weavers, it's the tanners!
Those price-war fanners! They should
   be tanned!
Give them their due!
Yes, I thought they would.
Up to nothing good!
More and more, the battle grows and
   grows!
You'll find butcher Klaus where there
   are rows!
Tomorrow is Friday!
There's fire in the house.
Look how he bruises!
Tailors with their gooses!
Guilds, join the fight! Soon 'twill be
   Friday!
Now let us have a try and hit a blow!
Get out of our way!
For we are here to stay!
Who are you that you should think that
   you can stop us?
Make way, we'll use our fists!
Tinkers! Coopers! Tinmongers! Glue-
   boilers! Pitchboilers!
Go away yourselves!
We won't give an inch!
No retreating! Cloth-shearers, sheet-
   weavers!
Over here, if you dare!
Let us pounce on them!

MASTERS

What is this noise and why this fight?
It spoils the quiet night!
Be still, go home and lie down, each one
   in his bed.
Or else it will be hailing on your head!
That's enough, now break it up!
Else we, too, will join the fight!
No way out, masters, join the fight.

MAGDALENE

Please listen, David!
I tell you, leave that man alone,
he meant no harm to me.

I tell you, let him be!
Hear, David ,are you mad?
It's Herr Beckmesser!

POGNER

(appears in his nightgown at the window)
Good Lord! Eva! Come in!
I'll see if downstairs all is safe.

WALTHER

No use despairing, we'll win by daring.
*(Walther presses with sword drawn to
the middle of the stage, to cut a way
for himself and Eva through the
alley. Sachs thereupon rushes vigor-
ously from his door, clears a way to
Walther swinging his strap and seizes
him by the arm.)*

POGNER *(on the steps)*
Hey! Lene! Where are you?

SACHS

*(pushing the almost fainting Eva up
the steps)*
Get in, Magdalene!
*(Pogner receives Eva and pulls her by
the arm into the house. Sachs draws
Walther with him into his house,
which he immediately closes behind
him. Neighbors, Prentices, Journeymen and Masters flee in all directions
so that the stage very soon becomes
empty.)*

NIGHTWATCHMAN

Listen to my word, good people.
It's now eleven on the steeple.
Beware of spectres and all that kind.
Let no evil ghost bewitch your mind!
Praise be God, our Lord!
*(As the Nightwatchman turns the cor-
ner, the curtain falls quickly with the
last chord.)*

ACT THREE

*In Sachs' workshop. In the rear the
half open door leading to street. On
the right side a chamber door. On the
left a window looking on the alley,
with flowers before it; on the same
side a work bench. Sachs sits in a
large arm chair at this window,
through which the morning sun shines
brightly upon him: he has a large
folio on his lap and is absorbed in
reading it.*

DAVID (*von der Strasse*)
Gleich Meister! Hier!
Die Schuh' sind abgegeben
in Herrn Beckmesser's Quartier.
Mir war's als rief't ihr mich eben?
(Er tut' als säh' er mich nicht?
Da is er bös, wenn er nicht spricht!)
Ach, Meister! woll't ihr mir verzeih'n;
Kann ein Lehrbub' vollkommen sein?
Kenntet ihr die Lene, wie ich,
dann vergäb't ihr mir sicherlich.
Sie ist so gut, so sanft für mich,
und blickt mich oft an so innerlich.
Wenn ihr mich schlagt, streichelt sie
    mich,
und lächelt dabei holdseliglich;
muss ich cariren, füttert sie mich,
und ist in allem gar liebelich.
Nur gestern, weil der Junker versungen,
hab' ich den Korb ihr nicht abgerun-
    gen.
Das schmerzte mich; und da ich fand,
dass Nachts einer vor dem Fenster
    stand,
und sang zu ihr, und schrie wie toll,
da hieb ich dem den Buckel voll.
Wie käm' nun da 'was Grosses drauf
    an?
Auch hat's uns'rer Liebe gar wohlgetan!
Die Lene hat mir eben alles erklärt,
und zum Fest Blumen und Bänder be-
    schert.
Ach, Meister! Sprecht doch nur ein
    Wort!
(Hätt' ich nur die Wurst und den
    Kuchen erst fort!)

SACHS (*sehr leise*)
Blumen und Bänder seh' ich dort?
Schaut hold und jugendlich aus.
Wie kamen mir die in's Haus?

DAVID
Ei, Meister 's ist heut festlicher Tag;
da putzt sich jeder, so schön er mag.

SACHS
Wär' heut' Hochzeitsfest?

DAVID
Ja, käm's erst so weit,
dass David die Lene freit!

SACHS
's war Polterabend, dünkt mich doch?

DAVID
(Polterabend?—Da krieg ich's wohl
    noch?)
Verzeiht das, Meister; ich bitt', ver-
    gesst!
Wir feiern ja heut' Johannisfest.

SACHS
Johannisfest?

DAVID
(Hört er heut' schwer?)

SACHS
Kannst du dein Sprüchlein, so sag' es
    her!

DAVID
Mein Sprüchlein? Denk', ich kann' s
    gut.
(Setzt nichts! Der Meister ist wohlge-
    mut.)
        (*laut*)
"Am Jordan Sankt Johannes stand"—

SACHS (*lächelnd*)
Was?

DAVID (*stellt sich gehörig auf*)
Verzeiht, Meister; ich kam in's
    Gewirr!
Der Polterabend machte mich irr.
"Am Jordan Sankt Johannes stand,
all' Volk der Welt zu taufen;
kam auch ein Weib aus fernem Land,
von Nürnberg gar gelaufen;
sein Söhnlein trug's zum Uferrand,
empfing da Tauf' und Namen:
doch als sie dann sich heim gewandt,
nach Nürnberg wieder kamen,
im deutschen Land gar bald sich fand's,
dass wer am Ufer des Jordan's
Johannes war genannt,
an der Pegnitz hiess der Hans."
Hans? Hans!
        (*feurig*)
Herr Meister! 's ist heut' eu'r Namens-
    tag!
Nein! Wie man so 'was vergessen mag!
Hier! Hier, die Blumen sind für euch,
die Bänder, und was nur Alles noch
    gleich?
Ja hier! schaut, Meister, herrlicher
    Kuchen!
Möchtet ihr nicht auch die Wurst ver-
    suchen?

SACHS
Schön' Dank, mein Jung'! Behalt's für
    dich!
Doch heut' auf die Wiese begleitest du
    mich:
mit Blumen und Bändern putz dich
    fein:
sollst mein stattlicher Herold sein!

DAVID
Sollt' ich nicht lieber Brautführer sein?
Meister! ach Meister, ihr müsst wieder
    frei'n!

DAVID (*coming from the street*)
Yes, master! Here!
The shoes I have delivered
in Master Beckmesser's home.
I heard that you called me?
(He acts as if I hadn't come.
He's always cross when he is mum!)
Forgive me, please, all the same:
can a prentice be without blame?
If you knew my Lene as I,
you would pardon me by and by.
She is so good, so soft to me;
her glance is as kind as kind as can be.
You use the belt,
she strokes my hair,
and all the while she smiles, meek and
    fair.
When I am fasting, she makes me eat.
In every way she is lovely and sweet.
Last night, though, since the knight
    was rejected,
she kept her basket; I felt neglected!
That gave me pain, what grieved me
    more:
I saw someone standing near her door:
He sang to her, he yelled and cried!
I went and tanned his tender hide!
Who cares if he was beaten up or not?
And for our love it has done a lot!
Now Lene told me how it all came to
    be,
and she gave flowers and ribbons to
    me.
Ah, Master, not one word you say?
(Wish that I could hide cake and saus-
    age away!)

SACHS (*very softly*)
Flowers and ribbons everywhere!
They look so young and so fair.
I wonder who put them there.

DAVID
Why, master, on so festive a day
we like to dress up as best we may.

SACHS
It's a wedding feast?

DAVID
If only it were that I should be wed to
    her!

SACHS
A bachelor party in advance?

DAVID
(Bachelor party? I don't have a
    chance!)
Forgive me, master, forget, I pray:
today we observe Midsummer Day!

SACHS
Midsummer Day?

DAVID
(Something is wrong.)

SACHS
You know your verses? Let's hear your
    song!

DAVID
My verses? Yes, I don't mind.
(I'm safe! The Master is meek and
    kind.)
    (*loudly and roughly*)
"St. John once stood on Jordan's
    bank . . ."

SACHS (*smiling*)
What's that?

DAVID
Forgive what I said:
that bachelor party turned my head!
"St. John once stood on Jordan's bank,
to baptize every human.
Among the folk from every rank
from Nürnberg came a woman.
She brought her son to the river's edge,
a blessed name she earned him,
and when she had fulfilled her pledge,
to Nürnberg she returned him.
When home she came, she found at
    once
that although where the Jordan runs
Johannes was his name,
on the Pegnitz it was Hans."
    (*considering*)
Hans? Hans! Ah! Master!
Your name is also Hans
and I forgot it, I'm such a dunce!
Here? All these presents are from me,
these ribbons, those flowers, all that you
    see.
This cake, look, master, it's full of
    spices!
Also this sausage . . . do taste some
    slices?

SACHS
No thanks, my boy. Put that away.
But down to the meadow I'll take you
    today.
With flowers and ribbons, neat and
    spruce,
you shall be in my herald's shoes!

DAVID
When you court let me be by your side.
Master, ah Master! You should take a
    bride!

SACHS
Hätt'st wohl gern eine Meist'rin im
Haus?

DAVID
Ich mein', es säh' doch viel stattlicher
aus.

SACHS
Wer weiss? Kommt Zeit, kommt Rat.

DAVID
's ist Zeit.

SACHS
Da wär' der Rat wohl auch nicht weit?

DAVID
Gewiss! Geh'n schon Reden hin und
wieder.
Den Beckmesser, denk' ich, säng't ihr
doch nieder?
Ich mein', dass der heut' sich nicht
wichtig macht.

SACHS
Wohl möglich; hab's mir auch schon
bedacht.
Jetzt geh und stör' mir den Junker
nicht.
Komm' wieder, wenn du schön gericht'!

DAVID
So war er noch nie, wenn sonst auch
gut!
(Kann mir gar nicht mehr denken, wie
der Knieriemen tut!) (ab)

SACHS
Wahn! Wahn!
Überall Wahn!
Wohin ich forschend blick'
in Stadt- und Welt-Chronik,
den Grund mir aufzufinden,
warum gar bis aufs Blut
die Leut' sich quälen und schinden
in unnütz toller Wut!
Hat keiner Lohn
noch Dank davon:
in Flucht geschlagen
wähnt er zu jagen;
hört nicht sein eigen
Schmerzgekreisch,
wenn er sich wühlt in's eig'ne Fleisch,
wähnt Lust sich zu erzeigen.
Wer gibt den Namen an?
s'ist halt der alte Wahn,
ohn' den nichts mag geschehen,
's mag gehen oder stehen!
Steht's wo im Lauf,
er schläft nur neue Kraft sich an:
gleich wacht er auf,
dann schaut, wer ihn bemeistern kann!
Wie friedsam treuer Sitten,
getrost in Tat und Werk,
liegt nicht in Deutschland's Mitten
mein liebes Nürenberg!
Doch eines Abends spat,

ein Unglück zu verhüten
bei jugendheissen Gemüten,
ein Mann weiss sich nicht Rat;
ein Schuster in seinem Laden
zieht an des Wahnes Faden:
wie bald auf Gassen und Strassen
fängt der da an zu rasen!
Mann, Weib, Gesell und Kind,
fällt sich da an wie toll und bind,
und will's der Wahn gesegnen,
nun muss es Prügel regnen,
mit Hieben, Stoss' und Dreschen
den Wutesbrand zu löschen.
Gott weiss, wie das geschah?
Ein Kobold half wohl da:
ein Glühwurm fand sein Weibchen
nicht;
der hat den Schaden angericht'.
Der Flieder war's: Johannisnacht!
Nun aber kam Johannistag!
Jetzt schau'n wir, wie Hans Sachs es
macht,
dass er den Wahn fein lenken mag,
ein edler Werk zu tun:
denn lässt er uns nicht ruh'n
selbst hier in Nürenberg,
so sei's um solche Werk',
die selten vor gemeinen Dingen,
und nie ohn' ein'gen Wahn gelingen.
(Walther tritt unter der Kammertüre
ein.)

SACHS
Grüss Gott, mein Junker! Ruhtet ihr
noch?
Ihr wachtet lang, nun schlieft ihr doch?

WALTHER (sehr ruhig)
Ein wenig, aber fest und gut.

SACHS
So ist euch nun wohl bass zu Mut?

WALTHER
Ich hatt' einen wunderschönen Traum.

SACHS
Das deutet Gut's: erzählt mir den!

WALTHER
Ihn selbst zu denken wag' ich kaum;
ich fürcht' ihn mir vergeh'n zu seh'n.

SACHS
Mein Freund! Das grad' ist Dichter's
Werk,
dass er sein Träumen deut' und merk'.
Glaubt mir, des Menschen wahrster
Wahn
wird ihm im Traume aufgetan:
all' Dichtkunst und Poëterei
ist nichts als Wahrtraumdeuterei.
Was gilt's, es gab der Traum euch ein,
wie heut' ihr sollet Meister sein?

SACHS

So you fancy a master with spouse?

DAVID

I mean, a wife does a lot for a house.

SACHS

Who knows, with time comes sense.

DAVID

It's time!

SACHS

Then sense, perhaps, is not far hence.

DAVID

That's true! Rumors set the city ringing;
that Beckmesser: surely, you can outsing
him!
Make sure he does not make a big to-
do.

SACHS

Yes, maybe. I had thought of that too.
Now go, and do not disturb our guest.
Come back, and wear your Sunday
best!

DAVID

He always is kind, but never like this!
(I can hardly remember any spanking
of his!)
(exit)

SACHS

Vain! vain! All things are vain
wherever I may look,
in every city's book,
the reason to discover
why people so delight
in torturing one another,
in such a furious fight.
No one wins gain or thanks from it;
a foe defeats him;
he thinks he beats him;
hears not the cries of his own dismay,
while his own flesh he tears away:
he fancies that is pleasure.
What works so great a feat?
The same old vain Deceit,
There's nothing done without it,
and no one dares to flout it.
If it should stop
to gather force, it sleeps a bit,
soon it wakes up,
then try if you can master it!
How peaceful, honor-founded,
so proud of deed and work,
by German lands surrounded
lies dear old Nürenberg!
And yet, one summer eve,

forestalling devastation
from passion's hot conflagration,
a man, holding no brief,
a cobbler, instead of cobbling,
sets old Deceit a-bubbling.
And soon through streets and through
places
Deceit in fury races!
Man, wife, a boy, a child
coming to blows as blind as wild!
And where Deceit is master,
there blows will rain the faster
with hitting, knocks, and maiming
to douse the fury's flaming.
God knows how that occurred!
A goblin said the word.
A glow-worm lost his wife that night,
that led to all that strife and fight.
The lilac scent . . . Midsummer night!
But now has come Midsummer Day!
Let's look now what Hans Sachs can do,
trying to guide that vain Deceit
to do some nobler deeds,
for, if Deceit proceeds
right here in Nürnberg,
then let it do such work
as seldom is by scoundrels nourished
and never without Deceit has
flourished!

(Walther enters by the chamber door.)

SACHS

Good day, my Stolzing!
Up at last!
You turned in late, but slept, I trust?

WALTHER
(very quietly)

Slept briefly, but my sleep was good.

SACHS

I find you in a happy mood?

WALTHER

I did have a wondrous, lovely dream.

SACHS

A splendid sign; let's hear it then.

WALTHER

I hardly dare to think of it,
for fear my dream may fade again.

SACHS

My friend, that is the poet's task,
the deeper sense of dreams to ask.
What may be mankind's true ideal,
that is what all our dreams reveal.
The verses that the poets wield,
they are the truth, by dreams revealed.
Who knows, my friend, this lovely
dream
may teach you yet a master theme.

WALTHER

Nein, von der Zunft und ihren Meistern
wollt sich mein Traumbild nicht
　begeistern.

SACHS

Doch lehrt' es wohl den Zauberspruch,
mit dem ihr sie gewännet?

WALTHER

Wie wähnt ihr doch nach solchem
　Bruch,
wenn ihr noch Hoffnung kennet!

SACHS

Die Hoffnung lass ich mir nicht min-
　dern,
nichts stiess sie noch über'n Haufen;
wär's nicht, glaubt, statt eu're Flucht
　zu hindern,
wär' ich selbst mit euch fortgelaufen!
Drum bitt' ich, lasst den Groll jetzt
　ruh'n!
Ihr habt's mit Ehrenmännern zu tun;
die irren sich und sind bequem,
dass man auf ihre Weise sie nähm':
wer Preise erkennt und Preise stellt,
der will am End' auch, dass man ihm
　gefällt.
Eu'r Lied, das hat ihnen bang ge-
　macht;
und das mit Recht: denn wohl bedacht,
mit solchem Dicht' und Liebesfeuer
verführt man wohl Töchter zum
　Abenteuer;
doch für liebseligen Ehestand
man and're Wort' und Weisen fand.

WALTHER

Die kenn' ich nun auch seit dieser
　Nacht:
es hat viel Lärm auf der Gasse ge-
　macht.

SACHS (*lachend*)

Ja, Ja! Schon gut! Den Takt dazu
hörtet ihr auch! Doch lasst dem Ruh'
und folgt meinem Rate, kurz und gut:
fasst zu einem Meisterliede Mut!

WALTHER

Ein schönes Lied, ein Meisterlied:
wie fass' ich da den Unterschied?

SACHS (*zart*)

Mein Freund! in holder Jugendzeit
wenn uns von mächt'gen Trieben
zum sel'gen ersten Lieben
die Brust sich schwellet hoch und weit,
ein schönes Lied zu singen
mocht' vielen da gelingen:
der Lenz, der sang für sie.

Kam Sommer, Herbst und Winterzeit,
viel Not und Sorg' im Leben,
manch' ehlich Glück danebben;
Kindtauf', Geschäfte, Zwist und Streit:
denen 's dann noch will gelingen
ein schönes Lied zu singen,
seht, Meister nennt man die!

WALTHER

Ich lieb' ein Weib und will es frei'n,
mein dauernd Ehgemahl zu sein.

SACHS

Die Meisterregeln lernt bei Zeiten,
dass sie getreulich euch geleiten,
und helfen wohl bewahren,
was in der Jugend Jahren
mit holdem Triebe
Lenz und Liebe
euch unbewusst in's Herz gelegt,
dass ihr das unverloren hegt.

WALTHER

Steh'n sie nun in so hohem Ruf,
wer war es, der die Regeln schuf?

SACHS

Das waren hochbedürft'ge Meister,
von Lebensmüh' bedrängte Geister:
in ihrer Nöten Wildnis
sie schufen sich ein Bildnis,
das ihnen bliebe
der Jugendliebe
ein Angedenken, klar und fest,
d'ran sich der Lenz erkennen lässt.

WALTHER

Doch, wem der Lenz schon lang
　entronnen,
wie wird er dem im Bild gewonnen?

SACHS

Er frischt es an, so gut er kann:
d'rum möcht' ich, als bedürft'ger Mann,
will ich die Regeln euch lehren,
sollt ihr sie mir neu erklären.
Seht, hier ist Tinte, Feder, Papier:
ich schreib's euch auf, diktiert ihr mir!

WALTHER

Wie ich's begänne wüsst' ich kaum.

SACHS

Erzählt mir euren Morgentraum.

WALTHER

Durch eu'rer Regeln gute Lehr'
ist mir's als ob verwischt er wär'.

WALTHER

No! of your guild, and its convention
the dream I dreamt has made no mention.

SACHS

It taught perhaps a magic word
to win them as a singer?

WALTHER

You know I failed when I was heard;
you know no hope can linger.

SACHS

I see no reason for dismay here;
myself, I go right on hoping;
if not, I, rather than make you stay here,
would have joined you and her, eloping;
and therefore, let your anger end.
You deal with worthy burghers, my friend.
They err at times, they like their ease,
expect that all will act as they please.
Whoever sets the rules,
and grants the prize, will choose
as winner one who satisfies.
Your song has filled them with doubt and fear,
as well it might! It would appear
that with a song of such ambition
you might lead our daughters to perdition.
But a man bent on a wedding ring
another tune and text would sing.

WALTHER

A song of that kind I heard last night,
a lot of noise in the streets left and right.

SACHS (*laughing*)

Yes, yes, that's true. You also know
some one marked the beat! But let that go
and do as I tell you. To begin
do attempt a master-song, to win!

WALTHER

A lovely song, a masterpiece . . .
What is the difference, tell me, please.

SACHS (*softly*)

My friend, while youth still weaves its spell,
while with a fervent power
first love begins to flower,
while hearts, impassioned, beat and swell,
to sing a song enchanted
to many then is granted,
for Spring sets words and tone.

Came summer, fall, and winter nights;
when often we are harried,
though happy to be married,
children, profession, strife, and fights—
only he who still untired
can sing a song inspired,
as master shall be known!

WALTHER

I am in love, I'll take a wife
to have a mate for all my life.

SACHS

The master-rules are there to guide you,
as truest friends they'll stand beside you,
and keep you, too, from squandering
what in your youthful wandering
in loving fashion,
spring and passion
laid unbeknownst to you in your heart.
With all that you must never part!

WALTHER

If now they are so highly prized,
by whom were all those rules devised?

SACHS

By some agrieved and doubting masters,
beset by life and life's disasters,
and through those tribulations
they fashioned their creations,
therein revealing
their youthful feeling,
a sweet remembrance, strong and true,
in which their spring could live anew.

WALTHER

Yet, if their springs lie far behind them,
how can they in their poems find them?

SACHS

They start afresh, as best they can:
I ask you, as a needy man,
teaching you rules as I knew them,
to show me how to renew them.
There is some ink here, paper, a quill:
I write, you sing, and trust my skill.

WALTHER

I hardly know how to begin.

SACHS

Just tell me what your dream has been.

WALTHER

Through all the rules that I have heard
it seems as though my dream were blurred.

SACHS

Grad' nehmt die Dichtkunst jetzt zur
Hand:
mancher durch sie das Verlorne fand.

WALTHER

So wär's nicht Traum, doch Dichterei?

SACHS

Sind Freunde beid', steh'n gern sich bei.

WALTHER

Wie fang' ich nach der Regel an?

SACHS

Ihr stellt sie selbst, und folgt ihr dann.
Gedenkt des schönen Traum's am
Morgen;
für's Andre lasst Hans Sachs nur
sorgen.

WALTHER

(*hat sich zu Sachs am Werktisch
gesetzt, wo dieser das Gedicht Walther's nachschreibt.*)
"Morgenlich leuchtend in rosigem
Schein
von Blüt' und Duft
geschwellt die Luft,
voll aller Wonnen,
nie ersonnen,
ein Garten lud mich ein,
Gast ihm zu sein."

SACHS

Das war ein Stollen; nun achtet wohl,
dass ganz ein gleicher ihm folgen soll.

WALTHER

Warum ganz gleich?

SACHS

Damit man seh',
ihr wähltet euch gleich ein Weib zur
Eh'.

WALTHER

"Wonnig entragend dem seligen Raum,
bot gold'ner Frucht
heilsaft'ge Wucht
mit holdem Prangen
dem Verlangen
an duft'ger Zweige Saum
herrlich ein Baum."

SACHS

Ihr schlosset nicht im gleichen Ton:
das macht den Meistern Pein;
doch nimmt Hans Sachs die Lehr'
davon,
im Lenz wohl müss' es so sein.
Nun stellt mir einen Abgesang.

WALTHER

Was soll nun der?

SACHS

Ob euch gelang
ein rechtes Paar zu finden,
das zeigt sich jetzt an den Kinden.
Den Stollen ähnlich, doch nicht gleich,
an eig'nen Reim' und Tönen reich;
dass man's recht schlank und selbstig
find',
das freut die Eltern an dem Kind:
und euren Stollen gibt's den Schluss,
dass nichts davon abfallen muss.

WALTHER

"Sei euch vertraut,
welch' hehres Wunder mir gescheh'n:
an meiner Seite stand ein Weib,
so hold und schön ich nie geseh'n;
gleich einer Braut
umfasste sie sanft meinen Leib,
mit Augen winkend,
die Hand wies blinkend,
was ich verlangend begehrt,
die Frucht so hold und wert
vom Lebensbaum."

SACHS (*gerührt*)

Das nenn' ich mir einen Abgesang:
seht wie der ganze Bar gelang!
Nur mit der Melodei
seid ihr ein wenig frei;
doch sag' ich nicht, dass das ein Fehler
sei;
nur ist's nicht leicht zu behalten,
und das ärgert unsre Alten!
Jetzt richtet mir noch einen zweiten
Bar,
damit man merk', welch' der erste war.
Auch weiss ich noch nicht, so gut ihr's
gereimt,
was ihr gedichtet, was ihr geträumt.

WALTHER

"Abendlich glühend in himmlischer
Pracht
verschied der Tag,
wie dort ich lag:
aus ihren Augen
Wonne saugen,
Verlangen einz'ger Macht
in mir nur wacht:
Nächtlich umdämmert der Blick mir
sich bricht;
wie weit so nah'
beschienen da
zwei lichte Sterne
aus der Ferne

SACHS

Put in the poet's art your trust:
through it you find what at first seemed
  lost.

WALTHER

It's not a dream then but poet's art?

SACHS

Those two are friends not far apart.

WALTHER

How do I start to please the school?

SACHS

To follow it, first *set* the rule.
Think of your morning dream in
  beauty,
the rest will be Hans Sachs' duty.
(*Walther has placed himself by the
workbench near Sachs who writes
down Walther's poem.*)

WALTHER

"Morning so radiant with rosiest ray,
a fragrance rare
has swelled the air,
and full of wonder,
come from yonder,
a garden bade me stay,
guest on my way."

SACHS

That was a stanza. Now take good care,
the second stanza must make a pair.

WALTHER

And why is that?

SACHS

For all to see,
you're choosing at once your wife-to-be.

WALTHER

"Wondrously gracious, in beauty un-
  told,
a blessed tree
appears to me,
a dream enchanted
I am granted:
its fragrant branches hold
fruit rich as gold."

SACHS

You ended in another key,
that makes the masters fret,
but thus you teach Hans Sachs to see:
in spring it must be like that.
Now let me hear an "after-song."

WALTHER

What does that mean?

SACHS

Your pair is strong:
the children they created
will show how well they're mated.
Though like the stanzas, not too much,
in tune and rhyme a special touch.
And if the child is neat and trim,
the parents' pride begins to brim.
Thus you conclude your stanza pair,
and nothing is left in the air.

WALTHER

"Let me confide what holy miracle I
  found:
I saw a woman fair and chaste;
by her delight my eyes were bound,
and like a bride
she folded her arms 'round my waist,
her eyes were shining,
her hands divining
what I had often craved to meet,
the fruit forever sweet
from life's green tree."

SACHS (*moved*)

That was an after-song, I will vow!
and one whole verse you've finished
  now!
Though with the tune, I admit,
you took your ease a bit,
but I myself do not find fault with it.
That it is hard to remember,
makes our fogies throw a temper!
And now you must sing yet a second
  verse,
so that 'we'll know which one was the
  first.
Nor did your rhymes tell,
though well-made they seemed,
what you imagined, what you have
  dreamed.

WALTHER

"Evening was greeting, in heavenly
  glow,
the dying day,
as there I lay,
her eyes enraptured
held me captured,
an all-embracing fire
woke my desire.
Night then enwrapped me,
my eyes broke in a trance:
from far and close
a light arose,
two stars were roaming
in the gloaming,

durch schlanker Zweige Licht,
hehr mein Gesicht.
Lieblich ein Quell
aus stiller Höhe dort mir rauscht;
jetzt schwellt er an sein hold Getön'
so stark und süss ich's nie erlauscht:
leuchtend und hell,
wie strahlten die Sterne da schön!
Zu Tanz und Reigen
in Laub und Zweigen,
der gold'nen sammeln sich mehr,
statt Frucht ein Sternenheer
im Lorbeerbaum."

SACHS
Freund! euer Traumbild wies euch
wahr:
gelungen ist auch der zweite Bar.
Wolltet ihr noch einen dritten dichten,
des Traumes Deutung würd' er berich-
ten

WALTHER
Wo fänd ich die? Genug der Wort'!

SACHS
Dann Tat und Wort am rechten Ort!
Drum bitt ich, merkt mir wohl die
Weise:
gar lieblich drinn sich's dichten lässt.
Und singt ihr sie im weit'ren Kreise,
so haltet mir auch das Traumbild
fest.

WALTHER
Was habt ihr vor?

SACHS
Eu'r treu'r Knecht
fand sich mit Sack und Tasch' zurecht:
die Kleider, drin am Hochzeitsfest
daheim ihr wolltet prangen,
die liess er her zu mir gelangen,
ein Täubchen zeigt' ihm wohl das
Nest,
darin sein Junker träumt.
Drum folgt mir jetzt in's Kämmerlein:
mit Kleidern wohlgesäumt
sollen beide wir gezieret sein,
wenn's Stattliches zu wagen gilt.
Drum kommt, seid ihr gleich mir
gewillt.
(*Er öffnet Walther die Tür und geht
mit ihm hinein.*)

BECKMESSER
(*lugt zum Laden herein; da er die
Werkstatt leer findet, tritt er näher.
Sein Blick fällt auf das von Sachs
zuvor beschriebene Papier auf dem
Werktische: er nimmt es neugierig
auf, überfliegt es mit immer grösserer
Aufregung und bricht endlich wüt-
end aus:*)
Ein Werbelied! Von Sachs! Ist's
wahr?
Ha! Jetzt wird mir alles klar!
(*Da er die Kammertüre gehen hört,
fährt er zusammen und versteckt das
Blatt eilig in seiner Tasche.*)

SACHS (*im Festgewande*)
Sieh da, Herr Schreiber: auch am
Morgen?
Euch machen die Schuh' doch nicht
mehr Sorgen?

BECKMESSER
Zum Teufel! So dünn war ich noch nie
beschuht;
fühl' durch die Sohle den feinsten
Kies!

SACHS
Mein Merkersprüchlein wirkte dies:
trieb sie mit Merkerzeichen so weich.

BECKMESSER
Schon gut der Witz, und genug der
Streich'!
Glaubt mir, Freund Sachs, jetzt kenn
ich euch!
Der Spass von dieser Nacht,
der wird euch noch gedacht.
Dass ich euch nur nicht im Wege sei,
schuft ihr gar Aufruhr und Meuterei!

SACHS
's war Polterabend, lasst euch bedeuten;
eure Hochzeit spukte unter den
Leuten:
je toller es da hergeh',
je besser bekommt's der Eh'.

BECKMESSER (*wütend*)
Oh, Schuster voll von Ränken
und pöbelhaften Schwänken.
Du warst mein Feind von je:
nun hör', ob hell ich seh':
die ich mir auserkoren,
die ganz für mich geboren,
zu aller Witwer Schmach
der Jungfer stellst du nach.
Dass sich Herr Sachs erwerbe
des Goldschmied's reiches Erbe,
im Meisterrat zur Hand
auf Klauseln er bestand;
ein Mägdlein zu betören,
das nur auf ihn sollt' hören,
und And'ren abgewandt,
zu ihm allein sich fand.

through tender branches danced
stars on my glance.
On peaceful height a lovely brook the
    quiet stirred,
with swelling tune it ran its way!
No sweeter sound I ever heard.
Beaming with light the stars had a spar-
    kle so gay!
Through boughs and branches,
alive with dances,
instead of golden fruit would boast
of golden stars a host
the laurel tree."

SACHS (*deeply moved*)

Friend, in your dream you weaved a
    spell,
you mastered the second verse as well.
If you care to let me hear another,
the dream's deep meaning we might
    discover.

WALTHER

But where to search? Enough was said!

SACHS

Put deed and song where they belong!
I beg you, don't forget that tune now,
a tune for poets' dreams to unfold.
When for the crowds you'll sing it soon
    now,
remember all that your dream has told.

WALTHER

What do you plan?

SACHS

Your faithful squire
put in a bag the right attire,
the clothes you chose, your very best,
to wear when you'd be married,
here to my house he had them carried.
A dove, perhaps, showed him to the
    nest
wherein his master dreamed.
Now follow me, let's go in there,
for raiments richly seamed
are the only ones we both can wear
on such a day of daring deeds!
Come on, if you agree with me.

(*Walther grasps Sachs' hand, who leads
him with a quiet, firm step to the
chamber door, opening it for him respectfully and then following him.*)

BECKMESSER

(*appears outside the shop window, looking in in great pertubation. Finding
the shop empty he enters hastily. His
glance falls on the paper with Sachs'*

*writing on it. He takes it up with curi-
osity, runs over it with growing excitement and at length breaks out in
fury.*)

A courting song! By Sachs? Can't be!
Ha! Now I begin to see.

(*He hears the chamber door open, starts
and hurriedly puts the paper in his
pocket.*)

SACHS (*in festive attire*)

It's you, friend Sixtus, what's your
    hurry?
It is not your shoes that cause you
    worry?

BECKMESSER

The devil! so thin none of my shoes
    have been!
Never I felt the stones before.

SACHS

For that you blame the Marker's chore:
only my marking made them so thin.

BECKMESSER

Do spare your wit and the tricks you
    spin;
It is too late to take me in.
Your jokes beneath the moon
I won't forget so soon.
To make sure I would not cross your
    path,
you caused an uproar; mutinous wrath!

SACHS

A bachelor party, what an occasion!
Your impending wedding caused a sen-
    sation!
The wilder that evening is,
the better for married bliss!

BECKMESSER (*furiously*)

Oh, cobbler, misbegotten!
Your pranks are truly rotten!
You always were my foe,
I'll prove that that is so!
The girl of my affection,
by destiny's selection,
all widowers' disgrace,
you've given her the chase.
So that Hans Sachs won't miss the
    chance
of Pogner's rich inheritance,
there, in the masters' school,
you pleaded every rule;
a maiden's brash seducer,
you said because you choose her
she must be wed to you!
No other man would do!

Darum! Darum!
Wär' ich so dumm?
Mit Schreien und mit Klopfen
wollte er mein Lied zustopfen,
dass nicht dem Kind werd' kund
wie auch ein And'rer bestund!
Ja, ja! Ha ha!
Hab' ich dich da?
Aus seiner Schusterstuben
hetzt' endlich er den Buben
mit Knüppeln auf mich her,
dass meiner los er wär'!
Au, au! Au, au!
Wohl grün und blau,
zum Spott der allerliebsten Frau,
zerschlagen und zerprügelt,
dass kein Schneider mich aufbügelt!
Gar auf mein Leben
war's angegeben!
Doch kam ich noch so davon,
dass ich die Tat euch lohn':
zieht heut' nur aus zum Singen,
merkt auf, wie's mag gelingen!
Bin ich gezwackt
auch und zerhackt,
euch bring' ich doch sicher aus dem
   Takt.

SACHS

Gut' Freund' ihr seid in argem Wahn;
glaubt was ihr wollt, dass ich getan,
gebt eure Eifersucht nur hin;
zu werben kommt mir nicht in Sinn.

BECKMESSER

Lug und Trug! Ich kenn' es besser.

SACHS

Was fällt euch nur ein, Meister Beckmesser?
Was ich sonst im Sinn geht euch nichts
   an;
doch glaubt, ob der Werbung seid ihr
   im Wahn.

BECKMESSER

Ihr säng't heut' nicht?

SACHS

Nicht zur Wette.

BECKMESSER

Kein Werbelied?

SACHS

Gewisslich nein!

BECKMESSER

Wenn ich aber d'rob ein Zeugnis
   hätte?

SACHS (*blickt auf den Werktisch*)

Das Gedicht? Hier liess ich's. Stecktet
ihr's ein?

BECKMESSER (*zieht das Blatt hervor*)

Ist das eure Hand?

SACHS

Ja, war es das?

BECKMESSER

Ganz frisch noch die Schrift?

SACHS

Und die Tinte noch nass?

BECKMESSER

's wär wohl gar ein biblisches Lied?

SACHS

Der fehlte wohl, wer darauf riet.

BECKMESSER

Nun denn?

SACHS

Wie doch?

BECKMESSER

Ihr fragt?

SACHS

Was noch?

BECKMESSER

Dass ihr mit aller Biederkeit
der ärgste aller Spitzbuben seit!

SACHS

Mag sein; doch hab' ich noch nie
   entwandt
was ich auf fremden Tischen fand;
und dass man von euch auch nicht
   übles denkt,
behaltet das Blatt, es sei euch geschenkt.

BECKMESSER

Herr Gott! Ein Gedicht? Ein Gedicht
von Sachs?
Doch halt', dass kein neuer Schad' mir
   erwachs'!
Ihr habt's wohl schon recht gut
   memoriert?

SACHS

Seid meinethalben doch nur unbeirrt!

BECKMESSER

Ihr lasst mir das Blatt?

SACHS

Damit ihr kein Dieb.

BECKMESSER

Und mach' ich Gebrauch?

To keep me numb
(I'm not so dumb!)
with shouting and with knocking
my song he would be mocking
so that she won't find out
that there's another about.
That's why! That's how!
I've caught you now!
And from your cobbler's corner,
your prentice's suborner,
you sicked your boy on me!
Good riddance I would be!
And thanks to you
I'm green and blue,
disgraced before the maid I woo!
You made him knock and thresh me
that no tailor can refresh me.
But I go further:
you planned on murder.
Luckily I got away,
your deed you shall repay.
Go on and sing this morning!
But let me give you warning!
It hit me hard,
but though I'm scarred,
I'll see to it that your beat is marred.

SACHS

My friend, you are indeed deceived.
I do not care what you believed,
though being jealous makes you blind,
yet courting I have not in mind.

BECKMESSER

That's a lie, you old transgressor!

SACHS

You're out of your mind, master Beckmesser.
If I have a plan, what's that to you?
But, friend, that I'm courting is quite
untrue.

BECKMESSER

You will not sing?

SACHS

Not competing.

BECKMESSER

No courting song?

SACHS

I tell you, no!

BECKMESSER

But what if I had some proof you're
cheating?

SACHS (*looks at the bench*)

Here it was . . . the poem,
where did it go?

BECKMESSER (*producing the paper*)

Is this from your hand?

SACHS

Ah . . . is that why?

BECKMESSER

The writing is fresh.

SACHS

. . . and the ink not yet dry.

BECKMESSER

Maybe, it's a biblical song?

SACHS

If that's your guess, your guess is wrong.

BECKMESSER

Well then?

SACHS

Well what?

BECKMESSER

You ask?

SACHS

Why not?

BECKMESSER

Despite your show of honesty
you seem the greatest rascal to me.

SACHS

Perhaps, and yet I was never known
to take away what I don't own.
And just so that no one might think you
  cheat,
the paper is yours, I give you that sheet.

BECKMESSER

Good Lord! Not that song? Not a song
  from you?
But wait . . .
I must watch for things I may rue.
You've learned those words by heart, I
  will bet?

SACHS

Believe me, my friend, you need not
  fret.

BECKMESSER

You give me the sheet?

SACHS

Your honor to save.

BECKMESSER

To use as I like?

SACHS

Wie's euch beliebt'.

BECKMESSER

Doch sing' ich das Lied?

SACHS

Wenn's nicht zu schwer.

BECKMESSER

Und wenn ich gefiel'?

SACHS

Das wunderte mich sehr!

BECKMESSER (*ganz zutraulich*)

Da seid ihr nun wieder zu bescheiden;
ein Lied von Sachs, das will was
    bedeuten.
Und seht nur, wie mir's ergeht,
wie's mit mir Ärmsten steht!
Erseh' ich doch mit Schmerzen,
das Lied, das Nachts ich sang,
dank eu'ren lust'gen Scherzen
es macht der Pognerin bang'.
Wie schaff' ich mir nun zur Stelle
ein neues Lied herzu?
Ich armer zerschlag'ner Geselle,
wie fänd' ich heut' dazu Ruh'?
Werbung und ehlich Leben,
ob das mir Gott beschied,
muss ich nun grad' aufgeben,
hab' ich kein neues Lied.
Ein Lied von euch, dess' bin ich gewiss,
mit dem besieg' ich jed' Hindernis:
soll ich das heute haben,
vergessen und begraben
sei Zwist, Hader und Streit,
und was uns je entzweit!
Und doch! Wenn's nur eine Falle wär!
Noch gestern war't ihr mein Feind,
wie käm's, dass nach so grosser Be-
    schwer'
ihr's freundlich heut' mit mir meint?

SACHS

Ich machte euch Schuh' in später
    Nacht:
hat man so je einen Feind bedacht?

BECKMESSER

Ja, ja! Recht gut! Doch eines schwört:
wo und wie ihr das Lied auch hört,
dass nie ihr euch beikommen lasst,
zu sagen, das Lied sei von euch verfasst.

SACHS

Das schwör' ich, und gelob' es euch:
nie mich zu rühmen, das Lied sei von
    mir.

BECKMESSER

Was will ich mehr. Ich bin geborgen:
jetzt hat sich Beckmesser nicht mehr zu
    sorgen.

SACHS

Doch, Freund, ich führ's euch zu
    Gemüte,
und rat' es euch in aller Güte:
studiert mir recht das Lied;
sein Vortrag ist nicht leicht;
ob euch die Weise geriet',
und ihr den Ton erreicht.

BECKMESSER

Freund Sachs, ihr seid ein guter Poet;
doch was Ton und Weise betrifft,
    gesteht,
da tut mir's keiner vor.
Drum spitzt nur fein das Ohr,
und: "Beckmesser,
keiner besser!"
Darauf macht euch gefasst,
wenn ihr mich ruhig singen lasst.
Doch nun memorieren,
schnell nach Haus:
ohne Zeit zu verlieren
richt' ich das aus.
Hans Sachs, mein Teurer,
ich hab' euch verkannt;
durch den Abenteurer
war ich verrannt.
So einer fehlte uns blos!
Den wurden wir Meister doch los!
Doch mein Besinnen läuft mir von
    hinnen!
Bin ich verwirrt, und ganz verirrt?
Die Silben, die Reime, die Worte, die
    Verse!
Ich kleb' wie am Leime, und brennt
    doch die Ferse.
Ade! ich muss fort.
An and'rem Ort
dank' ich euch inniglich,
weil ihr so minniglich;
für euch nur stimme ich,
kauf' eure Werke gleich,
mache zum Merker euch,
doch fein mit Kreide weich,
nicht mit dem Hammerstreich!
Merker! Merker! Merker Hans Sachs!
Dass Nürnberg schusterlich blüh' und
    wachs'!

(*Er hinkt, poltert und taumelt wie be-
sessen fort.*)

SACHS

So ganz boshaft doch keinen ich fand,
er hält's auf die Länge nicht aus:

SACHS

Just as you crave.

BECKMESSER

I sing what you wrote?

SACHS

If you succeed.

BECKMESSER

Suppose I should please?

SACHS

That would be strange indeed!

BECKMESSER

Now there you show too much modera-
tion.
A song by Sachs, that's quite a sensation.
No wonder that I am mad:
all the trouble I had!
I know, and I am choking,
the song I sang last night,
thanks to your cheerful joking,
it gave Fräulein Pogner a fright.
A new song that truly mattered,
that would be hard to find:
a poor man who's beaten and battered
has not enough peace of mind.
Marriage, a wife's devotion,
the blessing fate may bring,
I must give up the notion
if there's no song to sing.
A song by Sachs, I know what I say,
will conquer every stone on my way.
If I may have this writing,
there'll be no more fighting,
forget quarrels and woes
that ever made us foes.
And yet it could be a trap you set.
My foe you were all along.
Why should you suddenly now forget
and favor me with this song?

SACHS

To make your shoes, all night I slaved;
is that the way that your foes behaved?

BECKMESSER

Yes, yes! Quite so, but now you swear
that if you hear it sung somewhere,
you will never make any claim,
nor say that this song should bear your
name.

SACHS

I swear it. And I'll keep my word.
I'll do no boasting that I wrote the
song.

BECKMESSER

That's all I need! Troubles are over!
From now on Beckmesser will live in
clover.

SACHS

My friend, your passion must not blind
you,
therefore, allow me to remind you:
that song will try your wits;
to sing it is a chore,
to find the music that fits,
the melody to score.

BECKMESSER

Friend Sachs, to you as poet I bow,
but where tune and notes are con-
cerned, allow:
no rival need I fear.
So sharpen now your ear,
and: "Beckmesser—all are lesser!"
I am quite sure to please,
if you let me but sing in peace.
To learn it by heart now, home I run,
for I know, if I start now, it can be
done.
Hans Sachs! Good fellow! I have been
unkind,
but that reckless knight distracted my
mind,
he's one we could do without!
"Good riddance," we masters may
shout.
Madness has tinged me,
almost unhinged me.
I've gone astray,
I lost my way.
The words and the letters,
the rhyming, the scanning:
they hold me in fetters,
yet flames I am fanning!
Farewell! I must go.
But you must know:
thanks to your latitude
I'll change my attitude,
I'll show my gratitude,
buy of your works a set,
make you a marker yet,
but with the softest chalk,
not with a hammer stroke!
Marker! Marker! Marker Hans Sachs!
That Nürnberg may have the best of
lucks!
(*rushes limping and stumbling noisily
through the door*)

SACHS

Complete malice I'd yet have to find:
it's more than the vilest can bear,

vergeudet mancher ort viel Verstand,
doch hält er auch damit Haus;
die schwache Stunde kommt für jeden,
da wird er dumm, und lässt mit sich
reden.
Dass hier Herr Beckmesser ward zum
Dieb,
ist mir für meinen Plan gar lieb.
Sieh Ev'chen! Dacht' ich doch, wo sie
blieb'!

*(Eva, reich geschmückt und in glän-
zender weisser Kleidung tritt zum
Laden herein.)*

Grüss Gott, mein Ev'chen! Ei, wie
herrlich
und stolz du's heute meinst!
Du machst wohl Alt und Jung begehr-
lich,
wenn du so schön erscheinst.

EVA

Meister, 's ist nicht so gefährlich:
und ist's dem Schneider geglückt,
wer sieht dann, wo's mir beschwerlich,
wo still der Schuh mich drückt?

SACHS

Der böse Schuh! 's war deine Laun',
dass du ihn gestern nicht probiert.

EVA

Merk' wohl, ich hatt' zu viel Vertrau'n:
im Meister hab' ich mich geirrt.

SACHS

Ei, 's tut mir leid! Zeig her, mein
Kind,
dass ich dir helfe gleich geschwind.

EVA

Sobald ich stehe, will es geh'n;
doch will ich geh'n, zwingt's mich zu
steh'n.

SACHS

Hier auf den Schemel streck' den Fuss:
der üblen Not ich wehren muss.

*(Sie streckt den Fuss auf den Schemel
beim Werktisch.)*

Was ist's mit dem?

EVA

Ihr seht, zu weit!

SACHS

Kind, das ist pure Eitelkeit;
der Schuh ist knapp.

EVA

Das sagt' ich ja:

drum drückt er mich an den Zehen
da.

SACHS

Hier links?

EVA

Nein, rechts.

SACHS

Wohl mehr am Spann?

EVA

Hier mehr am Hacken.

SACHS

Kommt der auch dran?

EVA

Ach, Meister! Wüsstet ihr besser als ich,
wo der Schuh mich drückt?

SACHS

Ei! 's wundert mich,
dass er zu weit, und doch drückt
überall!

*(Walther, in glänzender Rittertracht,
tritt ein und bleibt beim Anblick
Eva's wie festgebannt stehen. Eva
stösst einen leisen Schrei aus und
bleibt ebenfalls unverwandt in ihrer
Stellung mit dem Fusse auf dem
Schemel.)*

EVA

Ah!

SACHS

Aha! hier sitzt's! Nun begreif ich den
Fall.
Kind, du hast recht: 's stack in der
Naht.
Nun warte, dem Übel schaff' ich Rat:
Bleib' nur so steh'n; ich nehm' dir den
Schuh
eine Weil' auf den Leisten, dann lässt
er dir Ruh'.
Immer schustern, das ist nun mein
Los;
des Nacht's, des Tag's, komm' nicht
davon los.
Kind, hör zu: ich hab' mir's überdacht,
was meinem Schustern ein Ende
macht:
am besten, ich werbe doch noch um
dich;
da gewänn' ich doch was als Poet für
mich.
Du hörst nicht drauf? So sprich doch
jetzt;
hast mir's ja selbst in den Kopf gesetzt!
Schon gut! ich merk': "mach' deine
Schuh'!"
Säng' mir nur wenigstens einer dazu!
Hörte heut' gar ein schönes Lied:
wem dazu wohl ein dritter Vers geriet'?

and though he squanders much of his
   mind,
he still has some to spare;
an hour of weakness finds him tender,
you play your game, and he will surrender.
The fact that Beckmesser stole that text
fits well what I am planning next.
It's Evchen! I was sure she would
   come!
(*Eva, richly dressed in gleaming white,*
   rather sad and pale, enters the shop
   and comes slowly forward.)
Good day, my Evchen! I admire you,
how proud you walk today!
You make both old and young desire
   you,
when you appear in this way.

EVA

Master, since when do you flatter?
My tailor had a success;
who cares then what may be the matter,
where still the shoe may press?

SACHS

The wicked shoe! It was your whim
that you refused to try it on.

EVA

Mind you, I put my trust in him,
the master, that I should not have done.

SACHS

Why, that's too bad. Come on, let's see.
That I may help you, one, two, three!

EVA

When I am standing, it may go;
but when I go, my foot says no.
(*She places one foot on the stool near*
   the bench.)

SACHS

Come, put your foot up, show your
   shoe:
there must be something I can do.
Now, what is wrong?

EVA

Too wide! You see.

SACHS

Child! That is sheerest vanity.
The shoe is tight.

EVA

Yes, yes, quite so.

It's tight and therefore it hurts my toe.

SACHS

Here left?

EVA

No, right.

SACHS

Up here maybe?

EVA

Rather in back there.

SACHS

It's unlikely.

EVA

Ah, master! Would you know better
   than I
where my shoe may pinch?

SACHS

I wonder why,
if it is large, it is everywhere tight!
(*Walther in his shining knight's costume*
   enters and remains, fascinated by the
   sight of Eva, standing motionless in
   the doorway. Eva utters a cry and
   remains in the same position, her foot
   on the stool, looking at Walther.)

EVA

Ah!!

SACHS

Aha! that's it: now I fathom your
   plight.
Child, you are right: something's amiss.
One moment and I'll take care of this.
Stay where you are; I'm sure that a last
is the thing that is needed; it will help
   you fast.
Always cobbling! that has been my fate:
by night, by day, both early and late.
But, my child, I have made up my
   mind;
I'll make an end of this cobbler's grind:
it's better that I should make you my
   wife,
and for once as a poet improve my life.
You pay no heed? I think you ought.
Was it not you who gave me that
   thought?
I see! you say: "stick to your shoe!"
Why does not somebody sing while I
   do?
Two lovely stanzas I have heard,
maybe some one would try to sing a
   third!

WALTHER

"Weilten die Sterne im lieblichen
Tanz?
So licht und klar
im Lockenhaar,
vor allen Frauen
hehr zu schauen,
lag ihr mit zartem Glanz
ein Sternenkranz."

SACHS

Lausch', Kind! Das ist ein Meisterlied.

WALTHER

"Wunder ob Wunder nun bieten sich
dar:
zwiefachen Tag
ich grüssen mag;
denn gleich zwei'n Sonnen
reinster Wonnen,
der hehrsten Augen Paar
nahm ich da wahr.
Huldreichstes Bild,
dem ich zu nahen mich erkühnt!
Den Kranz, von zweier Sonnen Strahl
zugleich verblichen und ergrünt,
minnig und mild
sie flocht ihn um das Haupt dem
Gemahl:
dort Huldgeboren,
nun Ruhmerkoren,
giesst paradiesische Lust
sie in des Dichters Brust
im Liebestraum."

SACHS

Derlei hörst du jetzt bei mir singen.
Nun schau', ob dazu mein Schuh
geriet?
Mein endlich doch es tät' mir
gelingen?
Versuch's, tritt auf! Sag', drückt er
dich noch?
Hat man mit dem Schuhwerk nicht
seine Not!
Wär' ich nicht noch Poet dazu,
ich machte länger keine Schuh'!
Das ist eine Müh', ein Aufgebot!
Zu weit dem einen, dem andern zu eng';
von allen Seiten Lauf und Gedräng':
da klappt's, da schlappt's, hier drückt's,
da zwickt's;
der Schuster soll auch alles wissen,
flicken was nur immer zerrissen:
und ist er nun Poet dazu,
da lässt man am End' ihm auch da
keine Ruh';
und ist er erst noch Witwer gar,
zum Narren hält man ihn fürwahr:
die jüngsten Mädchen, ist Not an
Mann,

begehren, er hielte um sie an;
versteht er sie, versteht er sie nicht,
all eins ob ja, ob nein er spricht,
am End' riecht er doch nach Pech,
und gilt für dumm, tückisch und frech.
Ei! 's ist mir nur um den Lehrbuben
leid;
der verliert mir allen Respekt:
die Lene macht ihn schon nicht recht
gescheit,
dass aus Töpf' und Tellern er leckt.
Wo Teufel er jetzt nur wieder steckt!

EVA

O Sachs! Mein Freund! Du teurer
Mann!
Wie ich dir Edlem lohnen kann!
Was ohne deine Liebe,
was wär' ich ohne dich?
Ob je auch Kind ich bliebe,
erwecktest du mich nicht?
Durch dich gewann ich
was man preist,
durch dich ersann ich,
was ein Geist!
Durch dich erwacht,
durch dich nur dacht'
ich edel, frei und kühn;
du liessest mich erblüh'n!
Ja, lieber Meister, schilt mich nur;
ich war doch auf der rechten Spur:
denn, hatte ich die Wahl,
nur dich erwählt' ich mir;
du wärest mein Gemahl,
den Preis nur reicht' ich dir.
Doch nun hat's mich gewählt
zu nie gekannter Qual;
und werd' ich heut vermählt,
so wär's ohn' alle Wahl:
das war ein Müssen, war ein Zwang!
Euch selbst, mein Meister, wurde bang.

SACHS

Mein Kind, von Tristan und Isolde
kenn' ich ein traurig Stück:
Hans Sachs war klug und wollte
nichts von Herrn Marke's Glück.
's war Zeit, dass ich den Rechten fand,
wär' sonst am End' doch hinein-
gerannt!
Aha! Da streicht schon die Lene um's
Haus:
nur herein! He, David! Kommst nicht
heraus?

(*Magdalene, in festlichem Staate, tritt
durch die Ladentür herein; aus der
Kammer kommt zugleich David,
ebenfalls im Festkleid, mit Blumen
und Bändern sehr reich und zierlich
ausgeputzt.*)

WALTHER

"Did not the stars dance a sweet roundelay?
and in her hair,
so light and fair,
to eyes admiring
and desiring
with every tender ray
the stars held sway."

SACHS

Such songs only a master knows.

WALTHER

"Wonder of wonders now fallen to my
part:
a twofold day
salute I may,
two suns of glory
rose before me:
from holy eyes a dart
pierced then my heart."

SACHS

That is the way that songs are sung
here!
Let's see if I have relieved your toes.
You will allow that there's nothing
wrong here?
Come on, stand up. Well, much better now?

WALTHER

"Image of grace,
that I had dared to hail and woo!
The wreath two suns had formed above,
though pale and faded, green anew,
loving and chaste
she twined it on the brow of her love:
in grace created,
to fame elated,
she pours the joys of the blest
into the poet's breast,
a lover's dream!"

SACHS

The man who makes shoes must be
quite insane!
If I were not a poet, too,
I would no longer make a shoe!
You work day and night, and all in
vain.
Too large for this one, too tight for the
next!
From every corner bothered and vexed!
It flaps, it snaps, it sticks, it pricks.
The poet, full of understanding,
patches anything that needs mending.
And if he is a poet yet,
that's but one more reason to chafe and
fret.

And worse, if he has lost his spouse,
they'll pull his leg in his own house:
the girls who are single, if men are
scarce,
will seek him for a husband, unawares!
He knows her heart, or knows it less;
who cares if he says no or yes!
They say: "Can't you smell the shoes?"
They call him dull, tricky, and loose.
Ah! that boy David: I'm sorry for him,
he has no respect left for me.
It's bad enough that he's caught Lene's
whim,
licking plates and dishes with glee.
The devil may know where he could be!

EVA

Oh, Sachs! My friend! My dearest one!
How can I thank you for all you've
done?
But for your love's endeavor,
what could I ever be?
A childish girl forever,
till you awakened me!
'Twas you who taught me what is right,
'twas you who brought me mind's delight,
'twas you who bade,
'twas you who made
me noble, free and true!
I blossomed forth through you!
Yes, master, chide me if you must,
my feeling yet was right, I trust,
for if my choice were free,
to you I should be true,
my husband you should be,
the prize would be for you.
My choice was made for me,
my torment ever grows;
if wife I am to be,
it was not I who chose:
by someone higher my choice was made!
You, too, my master, were afraid.

SACHS

My child: of Tristan and Isolde
a bitter tale they tell.
Hans Sachs was wise and wanted
none of what King Mark befell.
'Twas time I found the proper one,
or else, into the trap I might have run!
Aha! I see our Lene slinks about!
Come right in! Hey! David! Won't you
come out?

(*Magdalene, in festive array, enters
through the shop door. David, also
dressed for the festivities, decked out
with flowers and ribbons, comes out
of the chamber at the same time.*)

Die Zeugen sind da, Gevatter zur
    Hand:
jetzt schnell zur Taufe! Nehmt euren
    Stand!
(*Alle blicken ihn verwundert an.*)
Ein Kind ward hier geboren:
jetzt sei ihm ein Nam' erkoren.
So ist's nach Meisterweis' und Art,
wenn eine Meisterweise geschaffen
    ward,
dass die einen guten Namen trag',
d'ran jeder sie erkennen mag.
Vernehmt, respektable Gesellschaft,
was euch hier zur Stell' schafft!
Eine Meisterweise ist gelungen,
von Junker Walther gedichtet und ge-
    sungen:
der jungen Weise lebender Vater
lud mich und die Pognerin zu Gevatter;
weil wir die Weise wohl vernommen,
sind wir zur Taufe hierher gekommen.
Auch dass wir zur Handlung Zeugen
    haben,
ruf' ich Jungfer Lene und meinen
    Knaben.
Doch da's zum Zeugen kein Lehrbube
    tut,
und heut' auch den Spruch er gesungen
    gut,
so mach' ich den Burschen gleich zum
    Gesell';
Knie nieder, David, und nimm diese
    Schell'!
(*David is niedergekniet. Sachs gibt ihm
eine starke Ohrfeige.*)
Steh' auf, Gesell, und denk' an den
    Streich;
du merkst dir dabei die Taufe zugleich!
Fehlt sonst noch 'was, uns keiner schilt;
wer weiss, ob's nicht gar eine Nottaufe
    gilt.
Dass die Weise Kraft behalte zum
    Leben,
will ich nur gleich den Namen ihr
    geben:
"Die selige Morgentraumdeut-Weise"
sei sie genannt, zu des Meisters Preise.
Nun wachse sie gross, ohn' Schad' und
    Bruch.
Die jüngste Gevatterin spricht den
    Spruch.

QUINTETT

EVA

Selig, wie die Sonne
meines Glückes lacht,
Morgen voller Wonne,
selig mir erwacht!
Traum der höchsten Hulden,
himmlisch Morgenglüh'n!
Deutung euch zu schulden
selig süss' Bemüh'n!
Einer Weise mild und hehr,
sollt' es hold gelingen,
meines Herzens süss' Beschwer'
deutend zu bezwingen.
Ob es nur ein Morgentraum?
Selig deut' ich mir es kaum.
Doch die Weise,
was sie leise
mir vertraut,
hell und laut
in der Meister vollem Kreis',
deute sie auf den höchsten Preis!

WALTHER

Deine Liebe liess es mir gelingen,
meines Herzens süss' Beschwer'
deutend zu bezwingen:
ob es noch der Morgentraum?
Selig deut' ich mir es kaum.
Doch die Weise,
was sie leise
dir vertraut
im stillen Raum,
hell und laut,
in der Meister vollem Kreis',
werbe sie um den höchsten Preis!

SACHS

Vor dem Kinde lieblich hold,
mocht' ich gern wohl singen;
doch des Herzens süss' Beschwer'
galt es zu bezwingen.
's war ein schöner Morgentraum:
dran zu deuten wag' ich kaum.
Diese Weise,
was sie leise
mir anvertraut'
im stillen Raum,
sagt mir laut:
auch der Jugend ew'ges Reis
grünt nur durch des Dichters Preis.

DAVID

Wach' oder träum' ich schon so früh?
Das zu erklären macht mir Müh':
s' ist wohl nur ein Morgentraum?
Was ich seh', begreif' ich kaum.
Ward zur Stelle
gleich Geselle?
Lene Braut?
Im Kirchenraum
wir gar getraut?
's geht der Kopf mir, wie im Kreis',
dass ich Meister bald heiss'!

The witnesses there, the god-father is found;
now, for the christening, gather around!
(*All look at him in surprise.*)
A child has joined the living.
Let us find a name to give it.
Such are the masters' ancient ways:
whenever a master-tune we intend to praise,
we give it a good and honest name,
that every one may know its fame.
And now, my friends, you may ask me
what might our task be!
A master-tune has been presented,
that Walther Stolzing has written and invented,
the noble author of this creation
has asked both of us to a celebration.
And now the tune to which we've listened,
we have come here so it can be christened,
and since such an action needs a witness,
both Lene and David may prove their fitness.
But since as witness no prentice will do,
and since with his song I was satisfied, too,
a journeyman you are made now and here.
Kneel down here, David, take this on your ear.
(*David has knelt; Sachs gives him a loud box on the ear.*)
Get up, my boy, as journeyman arise,
this christening you won't forget in this wise.
There may be faults, but never mind:
this christening may be an emergency kind.
May the tune be strong, and stay among the living;
now listen to the name that I'm giving.
The "Most-blessed Morning Dream's True Story",
that be its name, to the master's glory.
And now may it grow, we wish it well,
as god-mother, Evchen here speaks the spell.

Quintet

EVA

Happy, as there yonder
smiles my fortune's sun,
morning, full of wonder,
happily begun:
dream of highest glory,
heavenly morning ray:
who can tell your meaning?
Happily sweet dismay!
To a beautiful, mildest strain
it may yet be granted
to reveal what sweetest pain
holds me all enchanted.
Was it but a morning dream?
Happy promise to redeem?
What that beauty has confided to my ear,
bright and clear
shall appear
when the masters will rise,
there to aim at the highest prize!

WALTHER

That you love me held me so enchanted
that the right to know my heart's
longing I was granted.
Is it still the morning dream?
Happy, dare I name its theme?
What its beauty has confided to your ear,
to you alone,
now is clear:
when the masters join and rise,
may it fight for the highest prize!

SACHS

Of the child, so mild and fair,
I would sing, enchanted,
but the right to tell my pain
I was never granted.
With this lovely morning dream
none may tamper, it would seem.
What its beauty
has confided,
softly, to my ears,
to me alone,
now is clear:
what in youth our heart decries,
blooms but through the poet's prize!

DAVID

Am I still dreaming, or awake?
That's a decision hard to make.
Perhaps . . . 'twas a morning dream?
I don't grasp the things I've seen!
Have you noted?
I'm promoted!
She—my bride?
We'll face the altar side by side?
I can see before my eyes:
as a master I'll rise!
Master—master!
soon I'll win that prize!

MAGDALENE

Wach' oder träum' ich schon so früh?
Das zu erklären macht mir Müh':
's ist wohl nur ein Morgentraum?
Was ich seh', begreif' ich kaum.
Er zur Stelle
gleich Geselle?
Ich die Braut?
Im Kirchenraum
wir gar getraut?
Ja, wahrhaftig! 's geht: wer weiss!
dass ich Meist'rin bald heiss'!

SACHS

Jetzt all' am Fleck! Den Vater grüss'!
Auf, nach der Wies', schnell auf die
    Füss'!

(*Eva und Magdalene gehen.*)

Nun, Junker, kommt! Habt frohen
    Mut!
David, Gesell': schliess' den Laden
    gut!

(*Als Sachs und Walther ebenfalls auf
die Strasse gehen, und David sich
über das Schliessen der Ladentüre
hermacht, wird im Proscenium ein
Vorhang von beiden Seiten zusam-
mengezogen, so dass er die Szene
gänzlich schliesst.—Als die Musik
allmählich zu grösserer Stärke ange-
wachsen ist, wird der Vorhang nach
der Höhe zu aufgezogen. Die Bühne
is verwandelt.*)

*Die Szene stellt einen freien Wiesen-
plan dar, im ferneren Hintergrunde
die Stadt Nürnberg. Die Pegnitz
schlängelt sich durch den Plan. Bunt-
beflaggte Kähne setzen unablässig die
ankommenden, festlich geschmückten
Bürger der Zünfte, mit Frauen und
Kindern, an das Ufer der Festwiese
über. Eine erhöhte Bühne mit Bänken
darauf ist rechts zur Seite auf geschlagen; bereits ist sie mit den Fahnen der angekommenen Zünfte aus-
geschmückt; im Verlaufe stecken die
Fahnenträger der noch ankommenden
Zünfte ihre Fahnen ebenfalls um die*
*Sängerbühne auf, so dass diese
schliesslich nach drei Seiten hin ganz
davon eingefasst ist. Zelte mit Ge-
tränken und Erfrischungen aller Art.*

DIE SCHUSTER (*indem sie aufziehen*)

Sankt Krispin, lobet ihn!
War gar ein heilig Mann,
zeigt', was ein Schuster kann.
Die Armen hatten gute Zeit,
macht' ihnen warme Schuh';
und wenn ihm keiner 's Leder leiht,
so stahl er sich's dazu.
Der Schuster hat ein weit Gewissen,
macht Schuhe selbst mit Hindernissen;
und ist vom Gerber das Fell erst weg,
dann streck', streck', streck'!
Leder taugt nur am rechten Fleck.

DIE SCHNEIDER

Als Nürenberg belagert war,
und Hungersnot sich fand,
wär' Stadt und Volk verdorben gar,
war nicht ein Schneider zur Hand,
der viel Mut hatt' und Verstand.
Hat sich in ein Bockfell eingenäht,
auf dem Stadtwall da spazieren geht,
und macht wohl seine Sprünge
gar lustig guter Dinge.
Der Feind, der sieht's und zieht vom
    Fleck:
der Teufel hol' die Stadt sich weg,
hat's drin noch so lustige Meck-meck-
    meck!
Meck! Meck! Meck!
Wer glaubt's, dass ein Schneider im
    Bocke steck'!

DIE BÄCKER

Hungersnot! Hungersnot!
Das ist ein gräulich Leiden:
Gäb' euch der Bäcker nicht täglich
    Brot,
müsst' alle Welt verscheiden.
Beck! Beck! Beck!
Täglich auf dem Fleck,
nimm uns den Hunger weg!

LEHRBUBEN

Herr Je! Herr Je! Mädel von Fürth!
Stadtpfeifer, spielt! Dass 's lustig wird!

DAVID

Ihr tanzt? Was werden die Meister
    sagen?
Hört nicht? Lass' ich mir's auch be-
    hagen.

MAGDALENE

Am I still dreaming, or awake?
That's a decision hard to make!
Was it but a morning dream?
I don't grasp the things I've seen!
He, I noted,
was promoted,
I—his bride?
We'll face the altar side by side?
All my friends will make big eyes,
when as mastress I rise.
I don't doubt it: he will soon be a
    master wise!

SACHS (to Eva)

All ready now? Greetings at home.
Off to the feast! Let us make haste.
    (Eva and Magdalene leave.)
Now, Stolzing, come: let's join the
    fight.
David, my boy, lock the shutters tight!

(As Sachs and Walther go together into
the street and David sets himself to
lock up the shop doors, a curtain is
drawn from both sides in the Proscenium closing in the scene.)

The curtains have been drawn up, and
a new scene represents an open meadow with the town of Nürnberg in
the distance. The Pegnitz, a narrow
stream, winds across the stage. From
gaily decorated boats, which arrive
continually at the bank, Burghers of
the Guilds, with women and children
in festive costume, land on the meadow. A raised platform with chairs
and benches has been erected on the
right, decked with the banners of
those Guilds which have already arrived. As new Guilds come on, their
banner-bearers also plant their banners around the platform so as finally
to close it in entirely on three sides.
Tents with drinks and refreshments
of all kinds.

In front of the tents there is merry
making; Burghers with women and
children and Journeymen sit and lie
about. Prentices of the Mastersingers,
richly decked with flowers and ribbons, with slender staves similarly
adorned, merrily act the parts of her-
alds and marshals; they receive the
new arrivals on the shore, order the
processions of Guilds and lead them
to the singers' platform, whence, after
the banner-bearers have planted the
banners, the Burghers and Journeymen disperse as they please. As the
curtain rises the Shoemakers are being thus received at the bank and
conducted to the foreground.

THE SHOEMAKERS

(advancing with flying banners)

Saint Crispin, Saint Crispin!
His is a saintly name:
for cobblers he won fame.
The poor thought him a friendly man,
he made them warming shoes,
when low his stock of leather ran,
he stole what he could use.
The cobbler's conscience is quite
    roomy:
he will make shoes though things look
    gloomy.
Take from the tanner what you can
    fetch,
and stretch, stretch, stretch!
Use your leather for shoes to stretch.

THE TAILORS

When Nürnberg was once besieged,
and famine plagued the land,
catastrophe would have been reached,
but for a tailor, a tailor, a tailor at hand
who was wise, and took a stand.
Sewed himself inside the skin of a goat,
then he took a walk right near the
    moat,
and there he strutted daily,
he jumped and bleated gaily.
The foe soon drew his forces back,
who wants a city, what the heck,
in which there are goats who sing
    meck, meck, meck!
Me-e-e-e-e-ck!
Who'd look for a tailor,
inside a goat?

THE BAKERS

Hunger pain! That we dread.
A famine spells disaster:
but for the baker and his daily bread,
the world would end much faster.
Bake! Bake! Bake!
Eating is at stake:
So bake us bread and cake.

PRENTICES

Look there! Look at the girls!
Town pipers, play! Let's dance away!

DAVID

You dance? But what if the masters
    knew it?
Rascals! Why should not David do it?

LEHRBUBEN
David! die Lene! die Lene sieht zu.

DAVID
Ach! lasst mich mit euren Possen in
Ruh'!

LEHRBUBEN
Die Meistersinger!

DAVID
Herr Gott! Ade, ihr hübschen Dinger!
(*Die Meistersinger ordnen sich am
Landungssplatze und ziehen dann
festlich auf, um auf der erhöh-
ten Bühne ihre Plätze einzunehmen.
Voran Kothner als Fahnenträger;
dann Pogner, Eva an der Hand führend; diese ist von festlich geschmückten und reich gekleideten
jungen Mädchen begleitet, denen
sich Magdalene anschliesst.*)

LEHRBUBEN
Silentium! Silentium!
Macht kein Reden und kein Gesumm'!
(*Sachs erhebt sich und tritt vor.*)

ALLES VOLK
Ha! Sachs! 's ist Sachs!
Seht Meister Sachs!
Stimmt an! Stimmt an! Stimmt an!
"Wach' auf, es nahet gen den Tag
ich hör' singen im grünen Hag
ein' wonnigliche Nachtigall,
ihr' Stimm' durchklinget Berg und
Tal:
die Nacht neigt sich zum Okzident,
der Tag geht auf von Orient,
die rotbrünstige Morgenröt'
her durch die trüben Wolken geht."
Heil Sachs! Hans Sachs!
Heil Nürnberg's teurem Sachs!

SACHS
Euch macht ihr's leicht, mir macht
ihr's schwer,
gebt ihr mir Armen zu viel Ehr'.
Soll vor der Ehr' ich besteh'n,
sei's mich von euch geliebt zu seh'n.
Schon grosse Ehr' ward mir erkannt,
ward heut' ich zum Spruchsprecher
ernannt.
Und was mein Spruch euch künden
soll,
glaubt, das ist hoher Ehren voll.
Wenn ihr die Kunst so hoch schon
ehrt,
da galt es zu beweisen,
dass, wer ihr selbst gar angehört,
sie schätzt ob allen Preisen.
Ein Meister, reich und hochgemut,
der will heut' euch das zeigen:
sein Töchterlein, sein höchstes Gut,

mit allem Hab' und Eigen,
dem Singer, der im Kunstgesang
vor allem Volk den Preis errang,
als höchsten Preises Kron,
er bietet das zum Lohn.
Darum, so hört und stimmt mir bei:
die Werbung steh' dem Dichter frei.
Ihr Meister, die ihr's euch getraut,
euch ruf' ich's vor dem Volke laut:
erwägt der Werbung selt'nen Preis,
und wem sie soll gelingen,
dass der sich rein und edel weiss
im Werben wie im Singen,
will er das Reis erringen,
das nie, bei Neuen noch bei Alten,
ward je so herrlich hoch gehalten,
als von der lieblich Reinen,
die niemals soll beweinen,
dass Nürenberg mit höchstem Wert
die Kunst und ihre Meister ehrt!
(*Grosse Bewegung unter allen. Sachs
geht auf Pogner zu.*)

POGNER
O Sachs, mein Freund! Wie dankens-
wert!
Wie wisst ihr, was mein Herz beschwert!

SACHS
's war viel gewagt; jetzt habt nur Mut!
Herr Merker! Sagt, wie steht's? Gut?

BECKMESSER
(*zu dem sich jetzt Sachs wendet, hat
schon während des Einzuges, und
dann fortwährend, eifrig das Blatt
mit dem Gedicht herausgezogen,
memoriert, genau zu lesen versucht,
und oft verzweiflungsvoll sich den
Schweiss getrocknet.*)
O! Dieses Lied! Werd' nicht d'raus
klug,
und hab' doch d'ran studiert genug.

SACHS
Mein Freund, 's ist euch nicht aufge-
zwungen.

BECKMESSER
Was hilft's? Mit dem meinen ist doch
versungen:
's war eure Schuld! Jetzt seid hübsch
für mich:
's wär' schändlich, liesst ihr mich im
Stich!

SACHS
Ich dächt', ihr gebt's auf.

BECKMESSER
Warum nicht gar?
Die andern sing' ich alle zu paar;
wenn ihr nur nicht singt.

PRENTICES

David! If Lene now came?

DAVID

Shush! I'm really sick and tired of your game!

PRENTICES

The Mastersingers!

DAVID

Good Lord! Farewell—I'll burn my fingers!

(*The procession of the Mastersingers has now reached the platform, where Kothner plants the banner: Pogner leading Eva by the hand. She is accompanied by girls gaily decked out and richly dressed; among them is Magdalene.*)

PRENTICES

Silentium! Silentium!
Not one word now, and not a hum.

CHORUS

There! Sachs! It's Sachs! Look: master Sachs!
Begin! Awake!
The dawn is near.
From verdant meadows a song I hear.
How wondrous sounds the nightingale!
Its voice is heard in hill and dale.
The night now bows to the western skies,
and day will soon in the east arise.
The dawn's red-glowing morning ray,
through darkest clouds now winds its way.
Hail! Hail to you, Hans Sachs!

SACHS

Joy fills your cries; doubt fills my heart,
if too much honor be my part.
Were so much honor my due,
it's but because I'm loved by you.
A signal honor came my way,
when I was named spokesman for this day.
You'll find, my speech, if you pay heed,
is in itself an honored creed.
If you have art so much at heart,
then you should learn with pleasure
that he who gives his life to art
esteems it past all treasure.
Of this, a master, rich and wise,
will give a demonstration,
his daughter's hand, the highest prize,
with all the wealth of his station
he'll offer as a proud award

to him who in the singers' art
pursues the highest aim
and wins the crowd's acclaim.
Now lend an ear, and you'll agree,
to court all poets must be free.
You masters who are bold and proud,
hear me before this festive crowd!
You see: the courtship's prize is rare,
whoever would be winner,
he must be pure and always fair,
as suitor and as singer,
if he would earn the guerdon
that never, since our art's creation,
was held in higher estimation
than by this bride intended,
who never shall lament it
that Nürnberg devotes her heart
to song and all her masters' art!

(*Great and general commotion. Sachs goes up to Pogner.*)

POGNER

Oh, Sachs! My friend, how very kind!
How well you know my heart and mind!

SACHS

We dared a lot:
now for the fight!
Friend Sixtus, say:
All's well? Right?

BECKMESSER

(*to whom Sachs now turns, has all through been constantly taking the poem from his pocket and trying to learn it by heart, often wiping the sweat from his brow in despair*)

Oh! What a song!
Can't make it fit,
and yet I've spent all day on it.

SACHS

My friend, you might as well refuse it.

BECKMESSER

My own would be worse still; I cannot use it.
It's all your fault! Now stay by my side,
to leave me would be worse than snide!

SACHS

I'd think you'd give up.

BECKMESSER

Most certainly not!
The others are an unworthy lot,
if you do not sing.

SACHS

So seht wie's geht!

BECKMESSER

Das Lied, bin's sicher, zwar keiner
    versteht;
doch bau' ich auf eure Popularität.

SACHS

Nun denn, wenn's Meistern und Volk
    beliebt,
Zum Wettgesang den Anfang gibt.

KOTHNER (*tritt vor*)

Ihr ledig' Meister! Macht euch bereit!
Der Ältest' sich zuerst anlässt.
Herr Beckmesser, ihr fangt an: 's ist
    Zeit!

BECKMESSER

Zum Teufel! Wie wackelig! Macht das
    hübsch fest!

DAS VOLK

Wie? Der? Der wirbt? Scheint mir
    nicht der Rechte!
An der Tochter Stell' ich den nicht
    möchte.
Der kann ja nicht 'mal stehn!
Wie soll es mit dem gehn?
Seid still! 'sist gar ein tücht'ger Meister!
Stadtschreiber ist er, Beckmesser heisst
    er.
Gott' ist der dumm!
Er fällt fast um!
Still! Macht keinen Witz;
der hat im Rate Stimm' und Sitz.

DIE LEHRBUBEN (*in Aufstellung*)

Silentium! Silentium!
Macht kein Reden und kein
    Gesumm'!

KOTHNER

Fanget an!

BECKMESSER

"Morgen ich leuchte in rosigem Schein,
von Blut und Duft
geht schnell die Luft;
wohl bald gewonnen,
wie zeronnen,
im Garten lud ich ein
garstig und fein."

DIE MEISTER (*leise unter sich*)

Mein! Was ist das? Ist er von Sinnen?
Woher mocht' er solche Gedanken ge-
    winnen?

VOLK

Sonderbar! Hört ihr's? Wen lud er ein?
Verstand man recht? Wie kann das
    sein?

BECKMESSER

"Wohn' ich erträglich im selbigen
    Raum,
hol' Gold und Frucht,
Bleisaft und Wucht:
mich holt am Pranger
der Verlanger,
auf luft'ger Steige kaum,
häng' ich am Baum."

DAS VOLK (*immer lauter*)

Schöner Werber! Der find't wohl seinen
    Lohn.
Bald hängt er am Galgen. Man sieht
    ihn schon!

DIE MEISTER

Was soll das heissen? Ist er nur toll?
Sein Lied ist ganz von Unsinn voll!

BECKMESSER (*immer verwirrter*)

"Heimlich mir graut,
weil es hier munter will hergeh'n:
an meiner Leiter stand ein Weib,
sie schäm' und wollt' mich nicht
    beseh'n:
bleich wie ein Kraut
umfasert mir Hanf meinen Leib;
mit Augen zwinkend
der Hund blies winkend,
was ich vor langem verzehrt,
wie Frucht so Holz und Pferd
vom Leberbaum."

(*Hier bricht Alles in lautes schallendes
    Gelächter aus. Beckmesser verlässt
    wütend den Hügel und eilt auf Sachs
    zu.*)

Verdammter Schuster! Das dank' ich
    dir!
Das Lied, es ist gar nicht von mir:
von Sachs, der hier so hoch verehrt,
von eu'rem Sachs ward mir's beschert.
Mich hat der Schändliche bedrängt,
sein schlechtes Lied mir aufgehängt.

(*Er stürzt wütend fort und verliert sich
    unter dem Volke.*)

VOLK

Mein! Was soll das sein? Jetzt wird's
    immer bunter!
Von Sachs das Lied? Das nähm' uns
    doch Wunder!

DIE MEISTERSINGER

Erklärt doch, Sachs! Welch ein
    Skandal!
Von euch das Lied! Welch eig'ner Fall!

SACHS

Das Lied, fürwahr, ist nicht von mir:
Herr Beckmesser irrt, wie dort so hier.

SACHS

Well, do your best.

BECKMESSER

The song, I'm certain, won't be understood;
but your popularity can stand the test.

SACHS

My friends, if the masters and you
allow,
our singing test may be started now.

KOTHNER (*advancing*)

You, single masters, are you prepared?
Proceedings by seniority!
Herr Beckmesser, you begin. It's time!

BECKMESSER

The devil! How rickety! Come fix it up!

CHORUS

What? He? He sings? Who would ever
choose him?
If I were the daughter, I'd refuse him!
He's falling down!
Lord, what a clown!
Be still! He is a valiant master.
He is the town clerk: Beckmesser,
Sixtus!
Why, I wonder if he wins.
He's shaky on his pins!
Still! None of your wit:
He has a seat where wise men sit.

PRENTICES

Silentium! Silentium!
Not one word now, don't even hum.

KOTHNER

Now begin!

BECKMESSER

"Mornings I radiate with rosiest ray,
a fracas rare
runs through the air.
It makes me wonder
how to plunder.
A garden made me stay,
ghostly and gay."

THE MASTERS

My! What is that? Is he demented?
What tale is this that our friend has
invented?

CHORUS

Very strange! You heard him. Who
made him stay?
How can that be? It's hard to say.

BECKMESSER

"Wandering spaces are sooty and cold,
a blasted tree
appeals to me:
a cream decanter
makes me banter,
its flagrant breezes scold,
I hang and hold."

CHORUS

What a singer! He'll get his due!
He'll swing from the gallows. That's
very true!

MASTERS

What does he drive at? He's lost his
mind?
His song is of the silly kind.

BECKMESSER

"I can't abide
when heinous spectacles abound!
I saw a woman, spare as paste,
and at my sight her eyes turned round,
pale as a hide.
She molded her charms round my
waist,
her eyes were winking,
her hounds were blinking,
what I had often craved to eat,
the fruit of wood and steed:
the liver tree!"
(*All break out into thundering laughter.
Beckmesser in fury leaves the mound
and rushes towards Sachs.*)
You wicked cobbler! That's what you
planned.
That song was never from my hand:
No. Sachs (who never has been wrong)
gave it to me: he wrote the song.
It made the scoundrel laugh with glee
to foist his rotten song on me.

(*He rushes away in fury and loses himself in the crowd.*)

CHORUS

My! What does he mean? Someone
made a blunder!
That song by Sachs? That would make
me wonder!

MASTERS

Explain yourself! What a disgrace!
You wrote that song? Peculiar case.

SACHS

My friends, I did not write that song.
Herr Beckmesser is, indeed, quite
wrong.

Wie er dazu kam, mag selbst er sagen;
doch möcht' ich nie mich zu rühmen
    wagen,
ein Lied, so schön wie dies erdacht,
sei von mir, Hans Sachs, gemacht!

MEISTER UND VOLK

Wie? Schön das Lied? Der Unsinns-
    wust?
Hört, Sachs macht Spass. Er sagt es
    nur zur Lust.

SACHS

Ich sag' euch Herrn, das Lied ist schön,
nur ist's auf den ersten Blick zu
    erseh'n,
dass Freund Beckmesser es entstellt!
Doch schwör' ich, dass es euch gefällt,
wenn richtig Wort und Weise
hier einer säng' im Kreise;
und wer dies verstünd' zugleich bewies',
dass er des Liedes Dichter,
und gar mit Rechte Meister hiess',
fänd er geneigte Richter.
Ich bin verklagt und muss besteh'n:
drum lasst mich meinen Zeugen auser-
    seh'n!
Ist jemand hier, der Recht mir weiss?
Der tret' als Zeug' in diesen Kreis!
(*Walther tritt aus dem Volke hervor.*)
So zeuget, das Lied sei nicht von mir;
und zeuget auch, dass, was ich hier
vom Lied hab' gesagt,
zuviel nicht sei gewagt.

DIE MEISTER

Ei, Sachs! Ihr seid gar fein!
Doch mag' es heut' geschehen sein.

SACHS

Der Regel Güte daraus man erwägt,
dass sie auch 'mal 'ne Ausnahm'
    verträgt.

DAS VOLK

Ein guter Zeuge, stolz und kühn!
Mich dünkt, dem kann 'was Gut's
    erblüh'n.

SACHS

Meister und Volk sind gewillt
zu vernehmen, was mein Zeuge gilt.
Herr Walther von Stolzing, singt das
    Lied!
Ihr Meister, lest, ob's ihm geriet.
(*Er gibt Kothner das Blatt zum
Nachlesen.*)

DIE LEHRBUBEN

Alles gespannt, 's gibt kein Gesumm:
da rufen wir auch nicht "Silentium!"

WALTHER

"Morgenlich leuchtend in rosigem
    Schein.
von Blüt' und Duft
geschwellt die Luft,
voll aller Wonnen
nie ersonnen,
ein Garten lud mich ein,
dort unter einem Wunderbaum,
von Früchten reich behangen,
zu schau'n im sel'gem Liebestraum,
was höchstem Lustverlangen
Erfüllung kühn verhiess—
das schönste Weib; Eva im Paradies."

DIE MEISTERSINGER

Ja wohl! Ich merk'! 's ist ein ander
    Ding,
ob falsch man oder richtig sing.

DAS VOLK

Das ist 'was and'res! Wer hätt's
    gedacht!
Was doch recht Wort und Vortrag
    macht!

SACHS

Zeuge am Ort, fahret fort!

WALTHER

"Abendlich dämmernd umschloss mich
    die Nacht;
auf steilem Pfad war ich genaht
zu einer Quelle reiner Welle,
die lockend mir gelacht:
dort unter einem Lorbeerbaum,
von Sternen hell durchschienen,
ich schaut' im wachen Dichtertraum,
von heilig holden Mienen,
mich netzend mit dem edlen Nass,
das hehrste Weib, die Muse des Par-
    nass!"

DIE MEISTER

s' ist kühn und seltsam, das ist wahr;
doch wohl gereimt und singebar!

DAS VOLK

Wie hold und traut so fern es schwebt;
doch ist's als ob man's miterlebt.

SACHS

Zeuge wohl erkies't!
Fahret fort und schliesst!

WALTHER

"Huldreichster Tag,
dem ich aus Dichter's Traum erwacht!
Das ich erträumt, das Paradies,
in himmlisch neu verklärter Pracht,
hell vor mir lag,

How he got the text, that's his own
　story,
I myself would never claim the glory
a song, so great and passing fine
should be thought to be one of mine.

MASTERS

What? Fine? All this nonsense brew?
Sachs makes fun of me and you.

SACHS

I tell you, friends, the song is great.
Only at one single glance one can state
that friend Beckmesser got it wrong.
Believe me! You will like the song,
if words and tune were mated
the way they were created.
And he who succeeds could also claim
that song was his creation,
and win the right to master fame
through just evaluation.
I am accused, I'll take the stand:
Thus let me choose a witness here at
　hand.
Is someone here who'll prove me wise,
Then as my witness let him rise.
(*Walther steps forward from the
　crowd.*)
Bear witness: that song bears not my
　name,
and witness, too, that what I claim
in praise of that song
was surely not too wrong.

MASTERS

Why Sachs, how very keen!
But wait until we've heard and seen.

SACHS

The rules and tenets we hold to be best,
are by exceptions put to the test.

CHORUS

A valiant witness, proud and trim!
Methinks good things may come from
　him.

SACHS

Masters and people now will ask
if my witness can fulfill his task.
Herr Walther von Stolzing, sing the
　song!
You, masters, please: do read along.
　(*He gives Kothner the paper to fol-
　low the song.*)

PRENTICES

Listen and hear! There is no hum!
And therefore we don't cry Silentium!

WALTHER

"Morning so radiant with rosiest ray;
a fragrance rare
has swelled the air,
and full of wonder,
come from yonder,
a garden bade me stay.
And there, beneath a wondrous tree,
where luscious fruits were thronging,
a dream of love appeared to me,
in answer to my longing.
It promised highest prize,
the fairest maid:
Eva—in paradise."

MASTERS (*murmuring softly*)

Why—yes! I see: that's another thing—
depending on the way you sing!

PEOPLE

That's very different! We have been
　wrong:
the way you sing it makes the song!

SACHS

Witness, well done—do go on!

WALTHER

"Evening had fallen, inviting the night;
on steepest crest
I found my rest;
and on the mountain
sprang a fountain
that lured with deep delight.
There, lying, 'neath a laurel tree,
through which the stars were gleaming,
a poet's day-dream came to me,
I saw a vision in my dreaming:
refreshing me with sweetest dews,
the noblest maid,
Parnassus sent its Muse!"

MASTERS

It's strange, and daring! That is true.
The rhymes are good for singing, too.

PEOPLE

How fair and sweet—it floats above:
and yet it reminds you of your love.

SACHS

Friend, whom well I chose,
do go on and close!

WALTHER

"Twice-blessed day,
that dawned upon a poet's dream!
The Paradise I longed to know
in Heaven's new transfigured gleam
shining it lay,

dahin lachend nun der Quell den Pfad
   mir wies;
die dort geboren,
mein Herz erkoren,
der Erde lieblichstes Bild,
als Muse mir geweiht,
so heilig ernst als mild,
ward kühn von mir gefreit,
am lichten Tag der Sonnen,
durch Sanges Sieg gewonnen
Parnass und Paradies!”

VOLK
Gewiegt wie in den schönsten Traum,
hör' ich es wohl, doch fass es kaum!
Reich' ihm das Reis, sein der Preis!
Keiner wie er zu werben weiss!

DIE MEISTER
Ja, holder Sänger: nimm das Reis;
dein Sang erwarb dir Meisterpreis!

POGNER
O Sachs! Dir dank ich Glück und Ehr';
vorüber nun all' Herzbeschwer!

EVA
Keiner wie du so hold zu werben
   weiss!
(*Sie erhebt sich, schreitet an den Rand
der Singerbühne und drückt auf die
Stirn Walther's einen Kranz.*)

SACHS
Den Zeugen, denk' es, wählt' ich gut:
tragt ihr Hans Sachs drum üblen Mut?

VOLK (*jubelnd*)
Hans Sachs! Nein! Das war schön erdacht!
Das habt ihr einmal wieder gut gemacht!

DIE MEISTER
Auf, Meister Pogner! Euch zum Ruhm,
meldet dem Junker sein Meistertum!

POGNER
(*eine goldene Kette mit drei Denk-
münzen tragend*)
Geschmückt mit König David's Bild,
nehm' ich euch auf in der Meister Gild'.

WALTHER
Nicht Meister! Nein!
Will ohne Meister selig sein!

SACHS
Verachtet mir die Meister nicht,
und ehrt mir ihre Kunst!
Was ihnen hoch zum Lobe spricht,
fiel reichlich euch zur Gunst.
Nicht euren Ahnen, noch so wert,
nicht eurem Wappen, Speer noch
   Schwert,

dass ihr ein Dichter seid,
ein Meister euch gefreit,
dem dankt ihr heut' eu'r höchstes
   Glück.
Drum denkt mit Dank ihr d'ran zurück,
wie kann die Kunst wohl unwert sein,
die solche Preise schliesset ein?
Dass uns're Meister sie gepflegt
grad' recht nach ihrer Art,
nach ihrem Sinne treu gehegt,
das hat sie echt bewahrt:
blieb sie nicht adlig, wie zur Zeit
wo Höf' und Fürsten sie geweiht;
im Drang der schlimmen Jahr'
blieb sie doch deutsch und wahr:
und wär' sie anders nicht geglückt,
als wie wo alles drängt und drückt,
ihr seht, wie hoch sie blieb in Ehr'!
Was wollt ihr von den Meistern mehr?
Habt Acht! Uns drohen üble Streich':
zerfällt erst deutsches Volk und Reich,
in falscher welscher Majestät
kein Fürst bald mehr sein Volk
   versteht,
und welschen Dunst mit welschem
   Tand
sie pflanzen uns in deutsches Land.
Was deutsch und echt wüsst' keiner
   mehr,
lebt's nicht in deutscher Meister Ehr'.
Drum sag' ich euch:
ehrt eure deutschen Meister!
Dann bannt ihr gute Geister;
und gebt ihr ihrem Wirken Gunst,
zerging' in Dunst
das heil'ge röm'sche Reich,
uns bleibe gleich
die heil'ge deutsche Kunst!

(*Während des folgenden Schlussge-
sanges nimmt Eva den Kranz von
Walthers Stirne und drückt ihn Sachs
auf; dieser nimmt die Kette aus Pogner's Hand, und hängt sie Walther
um. Nachdem Sachs das Paar um-
armt, bleiben Walther und Eva zu
beiden Seiten an Sachsen's Schultern
gestützt; Pogner lässt sich, wie hul-
digend, auf ein Knie vor Sachs nieder. Die Meistersinger deuten mit
erhobenen Händen auf Sachs, als
auf ihr Haupt. Alle Anwesenden
schliessen sich dem Gesange des
Volkes an.*)

VOLK
Heil Sachs! Hans Sachs!
Heil Nürnberg's teurem Sachs!

DER VORHANG FÄLLT.

and there, laughingly, the fountain bade
  me go,
from there descended,
my heart's intended,
the loveliest image ever seen,
my own inspiring muse,
so holy, mild of mien,
I dared to claim and choose.
I saw the morning sun arise,
I won the singer's highest prize:
Parnassus and Paradise!"

PEOPLE

A lovely dream has lulled my ear:
dimly I grasp the song I hear.
Give him his due: tried and true!
No one has wooed as well as you.

MASTERS

Yes, noble singer take your due:
Your song has shown you a master true!

POGNER

Oh, Sachs! You brought me peace and
  rest:
forgotten all that grieved the breast.

EVA

No one has ever wooed as well as you!
(*She bends down and crowns him with
a wreath of laurel and myrtle.*)

SACHS

My witness, grant me, proved my case:
are you annoyed with Sachs' ways?

PEOPLE

Hans Sachs—no! What a clever play!
And once again, Hans Sachs has won
  the day.

MASTERS

Now, master Pogner, for your fame,
grant Walther Stolzing the master
  name!

POGNER

(*turning to Walther, with a golden
chain adorned with three large
medals*)
King David's likeness tells you true,
the Master Guild has accepted you.

WALTHER

Not master! No!
Without you masters happiness I'll
  know.

SACHS

Don't ever scorn the master name,
and give their art its due!

All that has won them highest fame,
has richly favored you.
Not that your forebears stand the test,
that you own armor, sword and crest —
that you have poetry,
that masters grant your plea,
that is what brought you highest bliss!
With deepest thanks remember this:
how can an art be deemed so low,
if such a prize it can bestow?
That all our masters gave it care,
the way they thought it best,
in every weather foul or fair,
that kept it pure and blest:
though no more courtly as of yore,
when court and princes claimed its
  core;
when evil tempests blew,
German it stayed and true.
No other way it could survive
where all was full of stress and strife;
you see, its honor bore no stain.
What higher praise could masters gain?
Beware! Us threaten evil days:
if our great German realm decays,
when foreign powers rule the land,
no prince his people will understand,
if foreign sham and foreign lies
should ever darken German skies;
what's German and true could not
  abide
were't not for German masters' pride!
I beg of you: honor your German
  masters,
thus you will ban disasters!
And if you have their work at heart,
though fall apart
the Holy Roman Domain,
there still would remain
the holy German art!

(*During the following finale Eva takes
the wreath from Walther's head and
places it on Sachs, who takes the
chain from Pogner's hand, and hangs
it around Walther's neck. After Sachs
has embraced the pair, Walther and
Eva remain by his side leaning on his
shoulders. Pogner bends his knee as if
in homage before Sachs. The Mastersingers point with upraised hands to
Sachs as to their leader. All present
join in the song of the people.*)

ALL (*except Sachs*)

Hail! Sachs!
Our beloved Sachs!

END OF THE OPERA